Critical Guides to French Texts

75 Diderot: Supplément au Voyage de Bougainville

Critical Guides to French Texts

EDITED BY ROGER LITTLE, WOLFGANG VAN EMDEN, DAVID WILLIAMS

DIDEROT

Supplément au Voyage de Bougainville

Peter Jimack

Professor of French
University of Stirling

Grant & Cutler Ltd
1988

ISBN 0-7293-0297-0

I.S.B.N. 84-599-2542-0

DEPÓSITO LEGAL: V. 2.668 - 1988

Printed in Spain by
Artes Gráficas Soler, S.A., Valencia
for
GRANT & CUTLER LTD
55-57, GREAT MARLBOROUGH STREET, LONDON W1V 2AY

Contents

Contents

References

Quotations from the *Supplément* are from the Garnier Flammarion edition (Select Bibliography *7*), to which page numbers in parentheses refer. All other references, indicated in parentheses by italicized arabic numerals, are to the numbered items in the Select Bibliography.

For the reasons explained at the beginning of the Select Bibliography, I have used a variety of editions for quotations from works by Diderot other than the *Supplément*.

I have modernized eighteenth-century spelling in all cases.

1. Genesis

Louis-Antoine de Bougainville's *Voyage autour du monde par la frégate du Roi 'La Boudeuse' et la flûte 'L'Etoile'* was published in May 1771. The history of the voyage it recounts is bound up with that of eighteenth-century European colonialism, and more particularly with the complex origins of the disputed ownership of the Falkland Islands. The first French colonial empire was effectively destroyed by the treaty of Paris, which ended the Seven Years' War in 1763, and in the face of growing British expansion, there was some attempt in the ensuing years to seek new colonies. In 1764, Bougainville, who had already had a distinguished career as a soldier, having served with Montcalm in Canada, established a French settlement in the Falklands, with the aim of using it as a base for further exploration in the Pacific, and on 5 April, in his own words, 'je pris solennellement possession des îles au nom du roi' (*12*, p.83).

The following year, however, the British established a settlement on another island in the group, formally claiming them for the British crown. Meanwhile, Spain, who had been France's ally in the Seven Years' War and was now anxious to protect its South American possessions, urged France to cede the Falklands to them, and the French, concerned perhaps about the cost of maintaining the colony, agreed. Bougainville was the obvious person to be sent, first to Madrid to negotiate the deal, and then back to the Falklands to hand them over officially, a ceremony which took place on 1 April 1767.

But Bougainville had been quick to take advantage of this official mission and had obtained permission to use it as a starting point for exactly the kind of voyage of exploration he had had in mind in establishing the Falklands settlement in the first place. The voyage was in fact to last another two years, and Bougainville's ship *La Boudeuse* arrived back in Saint-Malo on

16 March 1769, having sailed through the Magellan Straits, across the Pacific, to the North of New Guinea and round the Cape of Good Hope.

By the time Bougainville's work appeared in print some two years later, public interest had already become focused almost exclusively on one aspect of the voyage, the apparent confirmation of the myth of the noble savage provided by the inhabitants of Tahiti, and more especially on their sexual mores. Bougainville's companions were not slow to recount the details of what must have been the high point of their arduous three years' voyage. As early as November 1769, the *Mercure de France* published a 'Post-scriptum sur l'île de la Nouvelle-Cythère' by Commerson, the naturalist of the expedition, who described Tahiti in unreservedly glowing terms as an 'Utopie [...] le seul coin de la terre où habitent des hommes sans vices, sans préjugés, sans besoins, sans dissensions' (quoted by Jacques Proust, *12*, p.22).

In any case, Bougainville himself had already pointed interest in this direction by bringing back to France with him a Tahitian called Aotourou, who was received by the King and became for nearly a year the darling of Parisian society. Reflecting the general enthusiasm, Bricaire de la Dixmerie published in 1770 an imagined harangue by Aotourou criticizing French morality, and although he was none too sure where exactly Tahiti was (he thought it was part of South America), his preface gives a good idea of the manner in which the ways of its inhabitants had captured the popular imagination: 'Il est vrai que les Mœurs Tahitiennes sont peu rigides; mais elles sont simples et vraies [...]. Ces Sauvages si bornés, ont pris la voie la plus courte pour arriver au bonheur. [...] L'Amour est leur besoin le plus fréquent, et ne leur coûte pas plus à satisfaire que d'autres. Nulle entrave ne gêne son essor. On dirait que cette Ile est uniquement consacrée à son culte' (*13*, pp.viii, x).

Bougainville's *Voyage*, when it was finally published, was on the whole impressively balanced, and he had clearly made a serious attempt to give an objective account of the evidence: on Tahiti, for instance, his first impressions were meticulously corrected by information gained from discussions with

Aotourou. But, as Proust has pointed out, Bougainville's readers 'ne lurent dans le *Voyage* que ce qu'ils s'attendaient à y trouver: une apologie du primitivisme et de l'amour libre, la condamnation de la propriété privée, et un exotisme discret qui ne les dépaysât point trop des chinoiseries de Boucher et des fêtes de Fragonard' (*12*, p.26).

This of course did not apply to Diderot. Even so, in the judicious review he wrote of Bougainville's book towards the end of 1771, his fascination with Tahiti was already apparent, and he even went so far as to say: 'Voilà le seul voyage dont la lecture m'ait inspiré du goût pour une autre contrée que la mienne' (*1*, II, p.206). The review, which was to become an early draft of the first two sections of the *Supplément*, the 'Jugement du Voyage de Bougainville' and the 'Adieux du Vieillard', was probably intended in the first instance for his friend Grimm's *Correspondance littéraire*, though it does not seem to have appeared in it. A year later, however, in October 1772, Diderot wrote to Grimm to thank him for the return of what must have been the review, making it clear that he was using it in the composition of what could only be the *Supplément* itself: '[hier] je regrattai un peu le troisième conte, qui était fait. Ainsi, le papier sur Bougainville est venu tout à temps' (*9*, XII, p.144).

The *Supplément* was in fact finished shortly afterwards, and appeared in the *Correspondance littéraire*, in four instalments, in September and October 1773, and March and April 1774 (see *30*, pp.384-85), to be published only in 1796. However, a few years before his death, probably in 1778 or 1779, Diderot revised his text, inserting a certain amount of new material, the most significant portion of which was the story of Polly Baker. A manuscript containing this revised version was discovered in Leningrad by Viktor Johansson (see *40*) and published in 1935 by Gilbert Chinard (*10*); it is this text which has formed the basis of subsequent editions, with the exception of Herbert Dieckmann's publication in 1955 of what seems to have been the original version of the work (*11*).

Now the reference in Diderot's letter to Grimm to 'le troisième conte' requires some explanation. Two weeks earlier (*9*, XII, p.131), he had given Grimm the manuscripts of two short stories, *Ceci n'est pas un conte* and *Sur l'inconséquence du jugement public de nos actions particulières* (sometimes known as *Madame de La Carlière*). Both these *contes* were circulated in 1773 in the *Correspondance littéraire*, and it has recently been discovered that when the *Supplément* also appeared in the *Correspondance* later that year, it was presented as the 'Suite des Contes de M. Diderot' (*30*, p.384). But even before this discovery (only in 1969), many critics had pointed out that various indications confirm that Diderot saw the two *contes* and the *Supplément* as forming a kind of triptych.

To begin with, the opening words of the *Supplément*, 'Cette superbe voûte étoilée, sous laquelle nous revînmes hier', clearly suggest a conversation following on from the one in *Sur l'inconséquence*, which ended with a reference to 'la nuit qui s'avance avec ce nombreux cortège d'étoiles' (*6*, p.835). But this continuity of décor serves to draw our attention to the more important thematic links which connect the *Supplément* to the two *contes* (and which have been analysed in detail by Dieckmann, *11*, pp.xciv-cxii). Diderot's intense interest in sexual morality and the problems associated with it had long been reflected both in his works – obvious examples are his two novels, *Les Bijoux indiscrets* (1748) and *La Religieuse* (1760) – and in his correspondence, especially the numerous letters to Sophie Volland. It has been suggested, plausibly enough, that it was Diderot's unhappy love affair with Mme de Meaux which led him to focus so particularly on the theme in 1772. *Ceci n'est pas un conte* and *Sur l'inconséquence* tell the stories of three couples (Mme Reymer and Tanié, Gardeil and Mlle de la Chaux in the first, Mme de La Carlière and Desroches in the second), all illustrating the terrible unhappiness that can be caused by conventional attitudes to sexual relationships, and more specifically by the importance attached to constancy and fidelity.

On the whole in the two *contes*, it is true, the authorial point of view appears to be rather different from that in the *Supplément*, and the victims of infidelity and inconstancy, it seems to me, are presented to us as tragic, or at least pathetic, rather than as misguided. But at the end of the second story, *Sur l'inconséquence*, there is a passage which suggests a rather different view of what has been recounted and manifestly looks forward to the *Supplément*: 'sans approuver les maris infidèles, je ne prise pas autrement les femmes qui mettent tant d'importance à cette rare qualité. Et puis j'ai mes idées, peut-être justes, à coup sûr bizarres, sur certaines actions, que je regarde moins commes des vices de l'homme que comme des conséquences de nos législations absurdes, sources de mœurs aussi absurdes qu'elles, et d'une dépravation que j'appellerais volontiers artificielle. Cela n'est pas trop clair, mais cela s'éclaircira peut-être une autre fois' (6, pp.834-35). The *Supplément* is therefore intended to complement the two *contes*, with the Tahitian utopia and the discussion of its implications counterbalancing the disasters narrated in the other two works.

The link is completed, both aesthetically and thematically, by a reference back to the two *contes* at the end of the *Supplément*, at a critical moment in the A-B discussion, immediately before B's important conclusion; in a passage which corresponds to the one just quoted from the end of *Sur l'inconséquence*, the characters of *Ceci n'est pas un conte* and *Sur l'inconséquence* are evoked as a pointed contrast to the good and happy Tahitians: 'Il est certain qu'on chercherait inutilement dans Tahiti des exemples de la dépravation des deux premiers, et du malheur des trois derniers' (p.185).

It is important, then, to bear in mind that the two *contes* constitute a kind of tacit preamble to the whole discussion of Tahiti in the *Supplément*. However, before we proceed to examine the thematic content of the work, it seems to me essential to give some consideration to its unusual form.

2. Structure and Form

The reader of the *Supplément* may well be thoroughly disconcerted by its somewhat fragmented form and continual changes of tone and manner, not to mention those of time and place. At the centre of the work is the double description of Tahiti, with a concomitant criticism of European mores and morality, in the form of the 'Adieu du Vieillard' and the conversation between the Tahitian Orou and Bougainville's chaplain, both allegedly written by Bougainville himself. The old man's speech, and a very solemn one it is, contrasts strikingly with the partly comic dialogue between Orou and the Aumônier, which was presumably supposed to have taken place some time earlier. These two sections are linked and, as it were, framed by the consequently fragmented dialogue between A and B, two somewhat philosophic Parisian gentlemen who offer a series of comments, first on Bougainville's *Voyage* itself, and then on these spurious additions to it, ending with a discussion of the lessons that Tahiti may or may not have for European society.

The work can thus be said to have a unity of form in that it appears as a series of interlocking dialogues. I include the 'Adieux', even though this is not strictly speaking a dialogue. The speech is undeniably dramatic in form: it is preceded and followed by virtual stage directions, and is addressed initially to the old man's own countrymen, though at the same time indirectly to the departing French, and then to the French directly, with the Tahitians as very involved bystanders; Tahitians and French are both silent participants in a quasi-dialogue. It must be said at this point that Diderot seems to have been or to have become virtually addicted to the dialogue or dramatized form. Quite apart from his actual plays, most of his works contain at least some sections of dialogue or conversation. His novel *Jacques le fataliste et son maître*, a first version of which certainly existed in 1771, consists, rather like the *Supplément*, of a complex interlocking series of dialogues and conversations. Indeed, the structure is made even more complex by the addition of an overall narrator, whose exchanges with an imagined reader constitute another interwoven dialogue. Other works, like *Le Neveu de Rameau* or the short *Entretien d'un père avec ses enfants* and *Entretien d'un philosophe avec la Maréchale de ****, are straightforward single conversations, with no narrative or editorial voice.

The conversations themselves may be used simply as a conventional narrative device. An innkeeper's wife in *Jacques le fataliste*, for example, tells Jacques and his master the long story of Mme de La Pommeraye, though this is broken up by various interruptions. At other times, the device is rather different: the authorial narrative in *Jacques* is turned into a dialogue by the introduction of a 'reader', an active narratee who continually challenges the narrator with questions and protests.

More frequently, however, the conversation takes the form of a more or less Socratic dialogue, with obvious didactic or philosophic intentions. But even in those dialogues in which one of the participants is Diderot himself, the technique varies. In the *Entretien avec la Maréchale*, for example, written less than two years after the *Supplément*, the Maréchale is a nice but rather silly and conventional woman who is shocked at Diderot's atheism and materialism, while the philosopher appears as the embodiment of good sense and even true virtue. In the *Entretien d'un père*, on the other hand, written a year or so before the *Supplément*, although 'Moi' is clearly Diderot, he is only *part* of him: as we shall see in a later chapter, neither 'Moi' nor his father emerges as a conclusive victor in their debate.

But this kind of philosophic dialogue finds its best expression in the *Neveu de Rameau*, which is a scintillating discussion between 'Moi', apparently Diderot, and 'Lui', the (historical) nephew of the composer, also called Rameau. The latter seems to be an amoral cynic, whose views are frequently presented as a frighteningly logical extreme case, argued from the very materialist principles which Diderot had himself advanced in other works; 'Moi' is left to marvel and be shocked, and to plead the cause of conventional virtue. Diderot critics have disagreed more completely about the interpretation of this work than about any other, but it seems to me difficult to deny that Rameau is in some measure a vehicle for Diderot's own thinking. The result is, in my view, a true dialogue, in which the component parts are complementary, as in the *Entretien d'un père*. To be understood properly, the dialogue must be viewed as a whole, and it is misguided in this case to seek Diderot's truth in only one of the interlocutors − as one can obviously do in the *Entretien avec la Maréchale*.

It is clear, then, that Diderot readily turned to dialogue to express his ideas, partly no doubt because this was rather how he himself proceeded intellectually, especially in his speculative thinking on highly controversial topics, namely by a series of hypotheses, objections and rejoinders. But partly also, I think, because he often found it impossible to come down with real conviction on one side of the debate rather than on the other, and out of intellectual honesty found himself compelled to present confrontation rather than conclusions. The result for the reader of Diderot is to make him a singularly elusive author, since associating himself with the opposing points of view in a dialogue was the equivalent of dissociating himself from both. It must be said, however, that purely as a literary device Diderot's use of the dialogue form was particularly successful: the alternation of different voices produces a liveliness and variety of tone in his best dialogues which make them very attractive reading − in contrast, incidentally, to the two (unsuccessful) plays he wrote in the 1750s, *Le Père de famille* and *Le Fils naturel*, which both suffer from a certain degree of monotony.

It is easy enough to see why the deliberately controversial subject matter of the *Supplément* should have lent itself to dialogue form, and also why an examination of the interlocking dialogues needs to precede consideration of the meaning of the work. The 'Adieux du Vieillard', to begin with, is obviously very different in form and tone from the A-B and Orou-Aumônier dialogues. It is openly presented as a set piece of eloquence which had been composed and written down beforehand, and it no doubt owed much to Diderot's early training in rhetoric at the Jesuit college in Langres. He was in fact rather fond of this kind of bravura passage, notable examples of which are to be found in his *Salons* and in the two plays already mentioned, and it is relevant to remember that the speech given in the *Supplément* to the old man had formed part of the original review of Bougainville's *Voyage*, where it was an apostrophe to Bougainville by Diderot himself. Perhaps the most interesting parallel with the 'Adieux', containing a similarly powerful element of pathos, is offered by the death-bed speech (another farewell) of the blind Cambridge mathematician, Saunderson, in the *Lettre sur les aveugles* (7, pp.103-06).

The old man's actual speech is framed by what is in effect a kind of stage direction, allegedly written by Bougainville. The introduction to the speech sets the tone with an evocation of the old man's previous stern response to the arrival of the French, characterized by the simple eloquence of dignified silence which the eighteenth century was inclined to see as the hallmark of primitive peoples: 'Son silence et son souci ne décelaient que trop sa pensée: il gémissait en lui-même sur les beaux jours de son pays éclipsés' (p.147). The speech itself begins, as it will continue, in a studied, rhetorical manner: 'Pleurez, malheureux Tahitiens! pleurez; mais que ce soit de l'arrivée, et non du départ de ces hommes ambitieux et méchants' (ibid.). Finally, the brief concluding 'stage direction' describes dramatically, and even poetically, the effect of the old man's rhetoric: 'A peine eut-il achevé, que la foule des habitants disparut: un vaste silence régna dans toute l'étendue de l'île; et l'on n'entendit que le sifflement aigu des vents et le bruit sourd des eaux sur toute la longueur de la côte: on eût dit que l'air et la mer, sensibles à la voix du vieillard, se disposaient à lui obéir' (p.151).

Although presented as part of the A-B dialogue, the account of the story of Polly Baker, a late and rather clumsily integrated addition to the text, is very much like the 'Adieux' in form: there is a similar brief introductory narrative, followed by a long (and equally implausible) similarly rhetorical speech, charged with pathos, and a short concluding paragraph to tell us how effective Polly's eloquence had been on her listeners. And obviously both speeches are meant to be taken absolutely seriously by the reader, which is to say that the figures of the Vieillard and Polly Baker are unambiguously sympathetic, and that their 'messages' are meant to appear, at least provisionally, as convincing to the reader as they are to their listeners. For a word of caution is necessary, particularly about the 'Adieux': while in one respect there is no ambiguity about the way in which Diderot means us to read the speech, it is only one element in the main debate of the work, the implications of Tahiti for European society, and so must still be considered in the context of the work as a whole.

The same is equally, though perhaps more obviously, true of the Orou-Aumônier discussion. The dialogue is introduced as forming part of a text supposedly written by Bougainville, and 'read' by B (though this is not entirely clear), but the narrative quickly establishes a tongue-in-cheek, mock-serious tone which is altogether different from the 'stage directions' framing the 'Adieu du Vieillard'. Any doubt we may have as to how we are to take the account of the chaplain's sexual temptations and fall must surely be dispelled by the way it is presented: 'le naïf aumônier dit qu'elle lui serrait les mains, qu'elle attachait sur ses yeux des regards si expressifs et si touchants; qu'elle pleurait; que son père, sa mère et ses sœurs s'éloignèrent; qu'il resta seul avec elle, et qu'en disant: Mais ma religion, mais mon état, il se trouva le lendemain couché à côté de cette jeune fille, qui l'accablait de caresses' (p.155). This seems to me frankly comic, being strikingly reminiscent of the brilliant first chapter of *Candide*.

The seriousness of the Aumônier's character is thus effectively undermined. Indeed, he frequently appears pretty much as a caricature, especially when he tries so feebly to justify himself to the implausibly articulate and intellectually sophisticated Orou: 'Que faites-vous donc? − Rien. [...] pourrais-tu m'apprendre le motif de la faveur et du respect que les magistrats vous accordent? − Je l'ignore' (pp.175,176). And to complete the picture, Diderot rounds the dialogue off, in a narrative paragraph, with a return to the sexual joke, as with reiterated cries of 'Mais ma religion! mais mon état!', the chaplain obligingly ('par honnêteté') goes to bed with the rest of Orou's womenfolk (pp.176-77).

The Orou-Aumônier discussion is not then a true philosophical dialogue of ideas, but anticipates rather the *Entretien avec la Maréchale*. Only one point of view is presented at all seriously, and we are expected to be convinced by it. However, the implications for European society of Orou's picture of Tahiti and his views on Christian morality are only hinted at in the dialogue; the serious discussion of these implications is quite another matter, and it is this that forms the substance of the next layer of the work, the debate between A and B.

This debate is certainly more of a philosophical dialogue, though only up to a point. A and B, as their 'names' suggest, are quite colourless, anonymous beings – unusually so for a Diderot dialogue – and they do not really express opposing viewpoints. It is obviously B who has all the best lines and who approximates most to Diderot; but A, instead of challenging him, merely asks the right questions, or else jumps to conveniently misguided conclusions, to be put right by B. The debate may not be as unbalanced as that between Orou and the Aumônier, but it is still one-sided, with A being little more than a 'stooge', and it can scarcely be seen as a dialogue of ideas on the model of the *Neveu de Rameau*. Nevertheless, it is a genuine intellectual exploration by means of the question and answer technique (hardly Socratic, since the one who asks the questions does not know the answers), which is obviously meant to be taken seriously by the reader.

Clearly, in looking for meaning in the *Supplément*, one must be careful about the precise status of what is said. In the absence of a direct authorial voice, or even an overall narrator, it would be most unwise, just as with a play, to take a statement by any one character to be expressing the views of the author. If B comes closest to Diderot, the meaning of the work must nevertheless be sought in the work as a whole, in the interplay of the interlocutors within each dialogue, and even more so, perhaps, in the interplay of the different sections with one another.

One can see then that the dialogue form in the *Supplément* corresponds to a stratification and juxtaposition of ideas in the work, and, as such, is in a sense inseparable from them. At the same time, the form of the work also has a purely 'literary' function, in providing a vivid and arresting presentation of the ideas and thereby contributing to the effectiveness of the debate. The discussion of ideas is further enhanced by the air of authenticity which seems to be achieved by the pretence that the two Tahitian episodes are contained in an unpublished manuscript addition to Bougainville's *Voyage* – with even, at one point, a marginal note written by the Aumônier himself - in rather the same way as Saunderson's dying speech in the *Lettre sur les aveugles* had also been allegedly taken from an unpublished manuscript.

Yet the device of the unpublished manuscript was so obvious and so hackneyed, even in the eighteenth century, that one hesitates as to how seriously it should be taken. As so often, it is difficult to distinguish between so-called realism and mock-realism. Diderot obviously did not really want the reader to believe that the two episodes had been written by Bougainville; the whole device is, rather, used playfully, and every now and again he reminds us that it is only a game. The reference to 'ce préambule qui ne signifie rien' (p.147) (which is presumably the discussion between A and B that has just taken place) is clearly humorous, and the comment by A that the old Tahitian's speech appears to contain 'des idées et des tournures européennes' (p.151), together with B's far-fetched explanation of how the speech came to be translated into French via Spanish, seems to me equally ludic. The technique is very like the one used in *Jacques le fataliste*, where continual (if playful) allegations of the truth of the narrative are accompanied by continual reminders – the pseudo-dialogues with the pseudo-reader, for example – that it is fiction.

The ultimate effect in *Jacques le fataliste*, however, is far from being the total destruction of realism. At the same time as he reminds us that it is all a fiction, Diderot lures the reader into believing, or almost, in the reality of the narrator-commentator, who is by no means omniscient and has very human lapses of memory. The realistic naturalism of the opening A-B dialogue, admittedly very rudimentary in comparison with *Jacques*, nevertheless seems to me to be aiming in this direction. It is true that a distinction must be made between the opening dialogue and its continuation, in which A and B become little more than ciphers and it is the ideas that take over. But in the early part, there is a lightness of tone created by the urbane facetiousness of worldly conversation (for example, the comments about Bougainville himself, p.142) which, instead of undermining the speakers – we are invited to smile *at* the chaplain, but *with* A and B – carries with it a high degree of credibility.

In any discussion of the ideas of the *Supplément* it is surely essential to bear in mind this variety and lightness of tone, though this does not make the discussion any easier, constituting as it does a warning not to take everything in the work too seriously. There is of course a danger here, and some commentators appear to have taken the warning so much to heart that they have been inclined to dismiss the *Supplément* as trivial and inconsequential. But a failure to take account of the changes of tone in the work has led to some over-solemn and unbalanced interpretations that I think are almost as mistaken.

3. 'La nouvelle Cythère'

The most immediately striking aspect of the *Supplément* for the modern reader is still surely the picture it gives of Tahitian sexual mores, just as much as it was for Diderot's contemporaries. Unfortunately, while academic critics have sometimes responded rather uneasily to this aspect of the work, it has often led other readers, who may well have read the *Supplément* with pleasure and/or amusement, to dismiss it as mild pornography which cannot be taken as a serious discussion of anything at all. It seems to me, however, desirable to focus briefly on the erotic element in the work, separately from the more general evocation of an earthly paradise of which it is obviously an integral part, if only because it does make such an impact on the reader. But this is not the main reason: I think we have to consider it seriously precisely because it constitutes such an important component of Diderot's critique of European morality, which I see as the principal purpose of the work.

In its essential elements, Diderot's picture of the sexual freedom of the Tahitians and their hospitality towards the French visitors is based faithfully on Bougainville's account. Bougainville had described how his men were welcomed by the islanders: 'On les invitait à entrer dans les maisons, on leur y donnait à manger; mais ce n'est pas à une collation légère que se borne ici la civilité des maîtres de maisons; ils leur offraient des jeunes filles; la case se remplissait à l'instant d'une foule curieuse d'hommes et de femmes qui faisaient un cercle autour de l'hôte et de la jeune victime du devoir hospitalier; la terre se jonchait de feuillage et de fleurs, et des musiciens chantaient aux accords de la flûte une hymne de jouissance. Vénus est ici la déesse de l'hospitalité, son culte n'y admet point de mystères, et chaque jouissance est une fête pour la nation' (*12*, p.235). If anything, Diderot toned down somewhat Bougainville's alluring picture, and when he deviated from it in other ways, it was obviously to set up the challenge to European morality. His version of Tahitian marriage, for example, would certainly not lead one to suspect that erring wives could, as Bougainville relates (*12*, p.258), be punished for their infidelity by death — although this was only when they erred without the husband's permission, which admittedly was not usually difficult to obtain.

Now to account for the appeal that Tahitian sexual behaviour seemed to hold for Diderot, reference has often been made to his own emotional life. By the time he wrote the *Supplément*, the early excitement of his marriage, contracted secretly and in defiance of his father's wishes some thirty years previously, had long since vanished, and there had for many years been a great deal of friction between him and his wife; his love affair with Sophie Volland seems to have been beset with all kinds of frustrations; and immediately before he wrote the *Supplément*, he was deeply involved in another, apparently abortive, affair with Mme de Meaux. After such complications, Diderot might well have envisaged rather wistfully some exotic place where, as the Aumônier put it, 'la passion de l'amour' was 'réduite à un simple appétit physique' (p.177) — though this scarcely tallies with the quasi-religious ceremonial involved in the civic celebration of the act of love that is described by both the Vieillard and Orou.

But there is surely no need to invoke Diderot's own experience of love and marriage to explain the attraction for him of this idyllic island, full of beautiful girls who offered themselves to the weary traveller, with open arms and, as it were, no strings attached! Bougainville made no bones about the effect on his men when the Tahitians first came on board: 'Ils nous pressaient de choisir une femme, de la suivre à terre, et leurs gestes non équivoques démontraient la manière dont il fallait faire connaissance avec elle. Je le demande: comment retenir au travail, au milieu d'un spectacle pareil, quatre cents Français, jeunes, marins, et qui depuis six mois n'avaient point vu de femmes?' (*12*, p.226). He went on to confess that he had found it just as hard to control himself as to control his crew.

Even for men who had not been at sea for six months but who

had merely been living subject to the normal restraints of European society, the picture of Tahiti might well seem to represent an enticing paradise, a veritable fantasy become reality. The yearning for this kind of sexual freedom is no doubt a fundamental psychological trait of civilized man, an ancient aspiration which has found expression in various myths throughout the ages. Bougainville tells us that they first called Tahiti 'nouvelle Cythère' (*12*, p.247), a reference to the Greek island (modern Kithira) which was one of the most potent expressions of the myth. It was the earliest Greek site of the worship of Aphrodite, who, according to Hesiod's version of the legend, had been born in the foam stirred up in the sea by the severed genitals of Uranus, and carried first to Cythera before stepping ashore in Cyprus. The symbol offered by this island devoted to the cult of Aphrodite has haunted the imagination of writers and artists in the modern world: among the most celebrated examples, one thinks of Watteau's use of the theme in his two great paintings, *Le Pélerinage à l'Ile de Cythère* and *L'Embarquement pour Cythère*, both dating from about 1717, and in a later century, Baudelaire's bitter poem, *Un Voyage à Cythère*, with its memorably characteristic line, 'Eldorado banal de tous les vieux garçons'.

At the same time, it must be remembered that there is a reciprocal influence between myth and life. If the myth was the expression of an aspiration, cultured men — like Bougainville as well as Diderot — could not avoid having their response to 'reality' shaped by their consciousness of the myth. As Yves Giraud has pointed out (*36*, pp.27-28), Bougainville carried his European cultural baggage around with him on his travels and interpreted what he saw accordingly. Whatever his response to Tahiti had been at the time, when he came to write his *Voyage* it appeared in many ways as a profoundly literary one. The description of his struggle to hold back his men, 'ces hommes ensorcelés', and to resist temptation himself, are strikingly reminiscent of Odysseus and the Sirens; and the association would seem to be confirmed by a reference to the origins of the Trojan War a few lines earlier, when the Tahitian girl who had come on board let fall her scanty garment 'et parut aux yeux de tous, telle que Vénus se fit voir au berger phrygien' (*12*, p.226).

Diderot's evocation of the sexual delights of Tahiti was also, by the same token, a profoundly literary one, though it no doubt had an equally valid psychological explanation. His source was Bougainville's perception of things rather than the reality which lay behind it, and to some extent he was merely participating in a literary tradition of which Bougainville's description of Tahiti had been the latest manifestation. And in Diderot's case, this seems to have been very much *en connaissance de cause*. While it is true that he was, for the most part, a consciously empirical thinker, he seems in this case to have been less interested in establishing the truth about Tahiti than in finding a conveniently idyllic portrayal of sexual mores to contrast with European conventions and to serve as a basis for a moral and philosophical discussion. When historical reality introduced a jarring note into the idyll, Diderot simply changed historical reality. When Bougainville delayed until after the description of Tahiti his revelation that his men turned out to have contracted syphilis from contact with the Tahitians, who must therefore have been already infected (see *12*, pp.271, 282), it could be argued that he was not guilty of distortion but was merely following the chronological order of events. Diderot, on the other hand, was consciously changing the facts, for obvious reasons, when his Vieillard accused the French of having infected the islanders.

As I pointed out earlier, Diderot had also rather obscured the facts about the sexual restrictions imposed on Tahitian women. In most respects, however, Bougainville's description of them lent itself perfectly to Diderot's sexual fantasy, and the latter did indeed follow him closely. The young girl offered to the French seemed to have little say in the matter, but was merely exhorted, the Vieillard says, to be 'complaisante et voluptueuse' as she served as a 'tendre victime du devoir hospitalier' (p.151), which is an almost verbatim echo of Bougainville's phrase (p.235, quoted above). According to Bougainville, 'les femmes doivent à leurs maris une soumission entière' (*12*, p.258), and Orou offers his wife and daughters to the Aumônier with the words: 'Elles m'appartiennent, et je te les offre' (p.154) (though he adds, it is true, 'elles sont à elles, et elles se donnent à toi'). In her article on the presentation of women in Diderot, Adriana Sfragaro has argued convincingly that according to both Orou and the Vieillard, woman in Tahiti was a 'femme objet', and she concludes: 'L'amour chez les indigènes n'est pas réciprocité, mais subordination de la femme à l'homme' (*45*, p.1898). If life in Tahiti seemed to correspond to a European sexual fantasy, it was undoubtedly a male fantasy, just as the myth of Cythera was essentially a male-orientated one, despite taking the form of the cult of a female deity.

No doubt this picture of subservient, compliant women is not presented by Diderot as a serious ideal. All the same, it contrasts oddly with the way in which, as I shall be discussing later, he laid stress on the sexual *freedom* of Tahiti which he opposed to the idea of marriage, based on possession. To this extent, then, his picture of Tahiti does seem to have been something of a self-indulgent erotic fantasy, which did not even fit in very well with the use he made of it as a way of attacking Christian morality; unless, that is, one accepts that woman's deepest aspiration is indeed to submit to the male, as Diderot perhaps implies by the 'elles sont à elles, et elles se donnent à toi'.

It is nevertheless difficult to avoid being anachronistic in making such comments, and it remains, I think, largely true that the sexual behaviour of the Tahitians is used by Diderot, not as an act of self-indulgence, and still less as a means of erotic titillation, but rather as the starting point for a serious debate about the basis of sexual morality, leading on to a discussion of social organization in general.

4. Primitivism and the Cult of Nature

Before we proceed to examine the more far-reaching aspects of the *Supplément*, it is important first to place the erotic element of the work in a somewhat wider context. The nostalgia for a sexual utopia was an aspect of, and to some extent symbolized, a more general nostalgia for some kind of utopian existence, a 'golden age', situated either in the remote past, or in some equally remote region of the world, and usually both, where people were perceived as living in something approaching their 'original' state. There were many examples of the myth in the ancient world, but in modern times, the proliferation of voyages of discovery in the seventeenth and eighteenth centuries added a new dimension to it, fuelling it with what often looked like, or what was made to look like, solid supporting evidence for the existence of such peoples. As travellers recounted their experiences in, say, North America or South-East Asia, the notion of a strong, healthy, simple (and therefore honest!) race of men began to crystallize into what became known as the myth of the noble savage or *bon sauvage*.

Of course, many of the accounts were pretty unreliable, among other reasons because explorers were often pre-conditioned to discover facts which matched the theories they already accepted, and this was probably even more true of those who read their accounts. We must bear in mind too, as Donald Charlton has recently reminded us (*18*, pp.118-23), that by no means everyone at the time accepted the noble savage myth: there were those who just as eagerly found evidence in the tales of the explorers to confirm their view of the baseness and depravity of modern savages, deprived as they necessarily were of the combined benefits of civilization and Christian grace — a view which was to be lent considerable support by the killing of Captain Cook in Hawaii in 1779.

Clearly, the response one had to the anthropological evidence was largely determined by one's religious, moral and political attitudes. The discovery of the noble savage was particularly convenient for those moralists who wished to castigate their contemporaries for their wickedness or foolishness, but without being committed to the Christian doctrine of original sin, with its concomitant of the fundamental corruption of human nature. The existence of a land in which people were so much better and happier than those one was familiar with offered an up-dated and corrected version of the Garden of Eden, in which the notion of irretrievably lost innocence was replaced by an attainable terrestrial ideal.

However suspect the actual evidence may have been, the myth appealed powerfully to the eighteenth-century imagination, and became one of the major themes of contemporary thought. More than anyone else, it was Rousseau who gave expression to it, particularly in his *Discours sur l'origine et les fondements de l'inégalité parmi les hommes* (1755), a work almost certainly considerably influenced by Diderot, who was still at that time a close friend of Rousseau's. In seeking to analyse the origins of the inequality which he saw as the source of men's unhappiness, Rousseau evoked the vision of a theoretical primitive state of nature in which man lived in isolation from his fellows, and then proceeded to describe the hypothetical successive stages which led to the creation of modern man in modern society.

Now both friends and foes alike tended to overlook, or at least blur, the distinction Rousseau had made between the true state of nature, in which man could not be seen as a moral being and was neither happy nor unhappy, and the primitive social group before its corruption by the arbitrary introduction of private property, the 'golden age' society in which man was both virtuous and happy. In fact, the word 'natural' was (and still is) used very loosely and with a variety of meanings: quite apart from the distinction just referred to between the pre-social and the primitive social, natural man in the historical sense means something very different from natural man in the psychological sense, and most writers in the eighteenth century tended to employ the phrase in both senses, often at the same time. But although the precise meaning of the term was often unclear, it was usually accompanied by the implication that what is natural is somehow good or right. Even though there were many who did not positively accept Rousseau's formulation that 'l'homme est naturellement bon', in practice, then as now, most people, including Diderot, seemed more or less to share this rosy view of 'nature', and it was principally the theologians who rejected it as constituting an explicit denial of the doctrine of original sin.

To some extent, Bougainville himself appears to have shared this general tendency to idealize natural man. At a time when the foundations of modern approaches to anthropology were only just beginning to be laid, it is scarcely surprising that, like other contemporary travellers and explorers, he was inclined to respond to what he saw under the influence of the prejudices of his century. But Bougainville was a more objective observer than most, and at various points in the *Voyage*, he showed that he had no idealistic illusions about the awful state of truly primitive natural man; indeed, Proust has seen the work as being 'd'une certaine manière l'antidote de Rousseau, ou plus exactement du «rousseauisme», tel qu'il s'était constitué au milieu du XVIIIe siècle' (*12*, p.21). During his arduous passage through the Magellan Straits, Bougainville had met a tribe of Indians whom he called 'Pécherais' and who were small, weak, ugly (the women were 'hideuses'), with decaying teeth, living in abject conditions in a horrible climate – and it was they who represented for him man in his natural state: 'De tous les sauvages que j'ai vus dans ma vie, les Pécherais sont les plus dénués de tout: ils sont exactement dans ce qu'on peut appeler l'état de nature' (*12*, p.192).

One could hardly imagine a more striking contrast than the subsequent description of Tahiti and its inhabitants. Here at last Rousseau's 'golden age' society of noble savages seemed to have been found. The idealization in Bougainville's account is evident enough. At one moment, he writes, 'Je me croyais transporté dans le jardin d'Eden' (*12*, p.235); at another, 'on croit être dans les champs Elysées' (*12*, p.249). There is little sign of 'nature red in tooth and claw': there are no snakes, and not even any troublesome insects; the soil is 'le plus fertile de l'univers' (*12*, p.236) and the climate is ideal.

The tone for the description of the inhabitants of Tahiti is set by the account of an incident which took place on Bougainville's first visit to the island: he and his companions sat and listened to an islander singing to the accompaniment of a flute, and the scene is described in terms of European culture — neatly revealing the ambivalence of the eighteenth-century response to primitive peoples — as being 'digne du pinceau de Boucher' (*12*, p.231). Indeed, the Tahitians seem at first to be beautiful, strong, healthy, peace-loving, and of course idyllically happy.

But are they? It soon transpires that, in a number of ways, the society of Tahiti was rather less ideal than at first appeared. To begin with, there were in reality two races of men on the island, and it was only one of these that was outstanding in stature and beauty. In addition, as well as infecting the French with syphilis, as we have seen, many of the islanders appeared to have had smallpox. But there were two aspects of Tahitian society, namely the existence of private property and of social inequality, in which Bougainville's self-correction seems particularly significant, for it will be remembered that these were both key elements in Rousseau's analysis of the corruption and unhappiness of modern European man. As far as the essentials of life were concerned, Bougainville reported that 'tout est à tous' (*12*, p.255), and that the Tahitians who were caught stealing from the French were punished merely by being thrashed. He went on to admit, however, that private property was in fact taken rather more seriously in Tahiti than he at first thought: 'mais j'ai su depuis [...] qu'ils ont l'habitude de pendre les voleurs à des arbres' (ibid). Similarly, although he had originally thought that the Tahitians were enviably happy, 'presque égaux entre eux, ou du moins jouissant d'une liberté qui n'était soumise qu'aux lois établies pour le bonheur de tous' (*12*, p.267), he subsequently realized that this was far from being the case: 'Je me trompais; la distinction des rangs est fort marquée à Taiti, et la disproportion cruelle' (ibid.). The inequality he then goes on to describe between 'les rois et les grands' and 'les gens du peuple' is about as far as one can imagine from an ideal state.

What is most striking in all this is that, as with the question of syphilis, Bougainville keeps in his text the initially idyllic picture, even though he afterwards goes on to show that he had been mistaken. The effect is to maintain the idealized portrait as the dominant statement, with the corrections appearing as little more than marginal comments.

It was no doubt the original, distorted account rather than the true facts about Tahiti that attracted Diderot. Certainly, the distortion suited his purpose very well, and it is the idealized portrait, with the corrective comments removed, that serves as the starting point for the *Supplément*. Instead of drawing attention to the discreet manipulation of truth in the *Voyage*, he either ignored altogether, or at least played down, Bougainville's reservations about the ideal state both of natural man in general and of the Tahitians in particular.

Diderot did, it is true, recognize in the preliminary A-B discussion that all savages are not necessarily like the Tahitians, but he simplified and exaggerated Bougainville's view of the goodness of natural man. When the savage behaves savagely, he argued, allegedly summarizing Bougainville, it is the fault of adverse circumstances: 'C'est, à ce qu'il paraît, de la défense journalière contre les bêtes féroces, qu'il tient le caractère cruel qu'on lui remarque quelquefois. Il est innocent et doux, partout où rien ne trouble son repos et sa sécurité' (p.145). Similarly, cannibalism and other barbarous practices resulting in population limitation, can be traced back to tribes living on small islands like the Ile des Lanciers (p.144). Diderot even admits that the Tahitians are capable of savage behaviour, but attributes this to the intervention of the Europeans in their society. It was only the Vieillard himself, he tells us, who dissuaded his fellows from killing Bougainville and his companions (p.150), but the massacre would have been in retaliation for the shooting of a Tahitian; and if the island's men envisage killing their contaminated wives and children, it would be to eradicate the poison of syphilis with which the French have infected them (p.149). In both cases the innocence of the Tahitians remains intact.

However, before the arrival of the French, Diderot claims,

circumstances in Tahiti had been entirely favourable, and his picture of the inhabitants is even more idyllic than Bougainville's. This is true above all of the Vieillard's version. All the islanders are handsome and well-built – with no mention of the two races. They are subject to no disease except old age – with no mention of smallpox, and with syphilis being expressly attributed to their French visitors. As for private property, the old man says, 'Ici, tout est à tous; et tu nous a prêché je ne sais quelle distinction du *tien* et du *mien*' (p.148) – and although this follows Bougainville to some extent, it makes no mention of his important subsequent correction. And finally, they are free and happy – with no reference whatsoever to Bougainville's revelation of their oppressive caste system, including the presence of slaves.

According to the Vieillard, the Tahitians, at least before the arrival of the French, were not only ideally happy and good, but also entirely *natural*, in a very precise sense: 'Nous suivons le pur instinct de la nature' (ibid.). This assertion seems, on the face of it, to be repeated by B in the 'Suite du Dialogue': 'je croirais volontiers le peuple le plus sauvage de la terre, le Tahitien qui s'en est tenu scrupuleusement à la loi de nature, plus voisin d'une bonne législation qu'aucun peuple civilisé' (p. 178). The claim that they are 'le peuple le plus civilisé de la terre' is an obvious exaggeration, presumably induced by the attractive paradox it sets up, and cannot be taken seriously. But 's'en est tenu scrupuleusement' is a revealing choice of words. B clearly implies that there had been a deliberate policy of self-restriction on the part of the Tahitians. A similar message is conveyed equally clearly in the 'Adieux': 'permets à des êtres sensés de s'arrêter, lorsqu'ils n'auraient à obtenir, de la continuité de leurs pénibles efforts, que des biens imaginaires' (p.149). No doubt it could be argued that the Tahitians' preference for 'repos' over work does constitute living according to 'la loi de nature', but it is difficult to see how such a conscious self-limitation could be seen as following 'le pur instinct de la nature'. And although we might have thought that at least their enjoyment of sexual intercourse was a clear case of following their natural instinct, the Vieillard assures Bougainville that they were motivated by the desire to 'enrichir la nation et la famille d'un nouveau citoyen' (p.150)! It is in the same spirit of duty to the general good that he reluctantly envisages sacrificing the women and children infected by the French to preserve the health of the nation.

The fact that Diderot's Tahiti represents a civilized society, however primitive, rather than anything that could possibly be termed a state of nature, is still more obvious, of course, in the somewhat different version of it given by Orou. Orou describes a community with laws, or at least conventions, aimed at the general good (precisely the kind of laws, incidentally, that Bougainville recognized the Tahitians did not have). The system of stimulating population growth and respect for the aged by an allocation of a portion of the community's wealth to the welfare of children and old people, the rules governing the use of chastity chains for boys (up to the age of twenty-two!), white veils for maidens and grey and black veils for non-fertile women, and the calculation involved in using the French visitors for stock-breeding purposes – all this indicates a thoroughly organized society, an even further cry from the Vieillard's 'pur instinct de la nature'.

Yet by criticizing European society for being contrary to nature, Orou implies that Tahitian society is, if not the state of nature exactly, at least in conformity with the laws of nature: 'Tu es en délire, si tu crois qu'il y ait rien, soit en haut, soit en bas, dans l'univers, qui puisse ajouter ou retrancher aux lois de la nature' (pp.158-59). And in the A-B discussion, to which we may reasonably turn for confirmation that this is in fact Diderot's view, we find B, as we have seen, referring to the Tahitian 'qui s'en est tenu scrupuleusement à la loi de nature'. So that although we may have left behind the Vieillard's simple notion of following 'le pur instinct de la nature', Diderot does seem to be suggesting that this society is organized in accordance with certain fundamental natural laws.

Is this then why it is good, as Orou seems to imply? Not so. A may appear inclined to believe, like the Vieillard, that what is natural is good and that the natural is to be preferred to the civilized, but B repeatedly corrects this simplistic view. He is no doubt thinking of something like Rousseau's hypothetical state of nature – or perhaps Bougainville's Pécherais? – when he refers to 'un état de l'homme triste et sauvage qui se conçoit et qui peut-être n'existe nulle part', and certainly not in Tahiti (p.181). But his refusal of a necessary link between natural and good is unequivocal. Nature is neither good nor bad, or rather it is both at once: 'Vices et vertus, tout est également dans la nature' (p.180). In other words, all human behaviour, good or bad, is ultimately natural, and the very concept of natural is therefore morally neutral.

Now 'nature' in this sense means something very different from the Vieillard's use of the term in his 'pur instinct de la nature'. Not only do we find the word used in the *Supplément* in (at least) two quite different ways, but we seem to be expected in the first instance to accept that the Tahitians are natural and therefore good; and subsequently to accept two radical correctives: one, that they are not in fact natural, and the second, that even if they were, they would not necessarily be good, since 'vices et vertus, tout est également dans la nature'.

Why then did Diderot leave such an obvious contradiction in the work, for there seems to be no suggestion that the Vieillard was in fact mistaken? There are, I think, two related explanations. Firstly, although Diderot did not naïvely think that all savages were *ipso facto* noble, he did accept, more or less, the Rousseauist thesis that what was natural was good, and that natural man was good in principle even when he was rather nasty in practice. As far as Tahiti was concerned, Diderot merely followed Bougainville, and if he took the idealization a little further, it was of a people who seemed, even without much distortion, to offer a marvellous confirmation of the existence of the 'bon sauvage'. For Diderot and his like-minded contemporaries, the words 'nature' and 'sauvage' had a prestige which automatically suggested goodness, even nobility.

It is this prestige which leads to the second explanation, for I suspect that, in some measure, Diderot was deliberately capitalizing on it. As I have already said, he was not concerned with anthropology for its own sake, and if he was interested in Tahiti, it was because it presented him with a golden opportunity for commenting on French civilization. The principal purpose of the *Supplément* is clearly to contrast Tahiti and France, with the intention of showing that the Tahitians are better and above all happier than the French. Like Rousseau once more, Diderot recognized that there were different degrees of civilization, and he presented the Tahitians as having, by their voluntary self-restriction, remained at a very early stage of it. This, of course, justifies to some extent seeing them as 'natural', since they are certainly closer to nature than the vastly more civilized French; but above all it is what has kept them good and happy, and certainly far better and happier than the French. Whether or not the Tahitians are natural is in the end perhaps a red herring, and the claim that they are seems to me to be used by Diderot largely as a dialectical device for reinforcing his more important claim that they are good and happy.

5. Christian Morality and European Society

Even before the 'Adieux du Vieillard', Diderot uses B as his *porte-parole* to herald the main drift of the work by establishing a striking contrast between Tahitian and European society: 'Le Tahitien touche à l'origine du monde, et l'Européen touche à sa vieillesse. L'intervalle qui le sépare de nous est plus grand que la distance de l'enfant qui naît à l'homme décrépit' (p.146). His choice of 'l'enfant qui naît' and 'l'homme décrépit' are clear enough indications of his preference. However, the first stage proper of the attack on European society is represented by the Vieillard's reproaches to the departing French, contrasting the wise self-restriction of the Tahitians with the Europeans' foolish development of unnecessary needs. Still closely following Rousseau, Diderot attaches great importance to the distinction between real and imaginary needs. The good society is one which is geared to the satisfaction of real needs, but there is a critical point beyond which these are increasingly supplemented by imaginary needs, and a vicious circle is set up; for the pursuit of 'des biens imaginaires' stimulates further desires: as B says, 'le terme du besoin passé, on est porté dans l'océan sans bornes des fantaisies, d'où l'on ne se tire plus' (pp.177-78). The Vieillard can thus declare: 'Tout ce qui nous est nécessaire et bon, nous le possédons' – whereas he sees the French as tormented by their 'besoins factices' and 'vertus chimériques' (pp.148-49).

In the A-B discussion, Diderot suggests an explanation for the development of these 'besoins factices'. Once man's ingenuity has been stimulated by, for instance, an infertile soil, this ingenuity can no longer be checked (p.177). And it is suggested that, rather than having restricted themselves by deliberate choice, as the Vieillard implies, the Tahitians may just have been very lucky, benefiting from a fortunate combination of natural indolence and a favourable soil and climate (in which case, of course, the French might be seen as just rather unlucky!). However, in the considerably more polemical 'Adieux', the key factor in this critical degeneration of society seems to be the introduction of private property, just as it is in Rousseau's *Discours sur l'inégalité*. The obsession of the French visitors with the distinction between *tien* and *mien* illustrates the way in which the moral degradation comes about: 'A peine t'es-tu montré parmi eux, qu'ils sont devenus voleurs. A peine es-tu descendu dans notre terre qu'elle a fumé de sang' (p.150). Since the Tahitians (allegedly) have no notion of private property, they naturally 'steal' from the French, and because the latter attach excessive importance to their 'méprisables bagatelles' (p.148), they barbarously kill one of the culprits; as a result, it was only the intervention of the Vieillard that saved the French from being massacred in their turn.

But as the Vieillard points out, the petty thefts committed by the Tahitians are as nothing compared with the theft of their country perpetrated by the French. The plaque they set up proclaiming 'Ce pays est à nous' was for the Vieillard 'le titre de notre futur esclavage' (p.148). Now to some extent, this discussion of colonialism and slavery was a digression in the *Supplément*, not referred to subsequently, and its association with private property is perhaps a bit contrived, no matter how good a debating point it makes. But unlike the debate in the rest of the work, which is mostly speculative and theoretical, Diderot is here commenting on a real contemporary issue, on which he himself felt very strongly. The discussion of Bougainville's *Voyage* afforded him an excellent opportunity to voice the detestation of colonialism and slavery – the two were often inseparable in the eighteenth century – which he developed elsewhere, particularly in his contributions to Raynal's *Histoire des deux Indes*.

Here, he presents colonialism and slavery as a totally unjustifiable extension of private property, unjustifiable even according to the (suspect) principles of the French, who could claim no rights over the Tahitians. In a more pointed allusion to contemporary issues, the Vieillard warned his compatriots what lay in store for them: 'Un jour, ils reviendront, le morceau de bois que vous voyez attaché à la ceinture de celui-ci, dans une main, et le fer qui pend au côté de celui-là, dans l'autre, vous enchaîner, vous égorger' (p.147). This reference to the crucifix and the role of the Church in colonialization had already been explained a few pages previously, in the A-B discussion of the *Voyage*. Although Bougainville had written at some length about the much-criticized despotic regime of the Jesuits in Paraguay – one recalls Voltaire's memorable formula in *Candide*, 'Los Padres y ont tout, et les peuples rien' (*16*, p.167) – he himself had contrived to sit on the fence on the subject; B, however, credited him by implication with what was obviously Diderot's own denunciation of the Jesuits' savage oppression of the Indians (pp.144-45).

Apart from their attitude to private property, the other main complaint the Vieillard has against the French, and the one which introduces the principal theme of the work, concerns their sexual behaviour. I have already referred to the question of syphilis, which he accused the French of having brought to the island: but even if this were true, it would not exactly have made the French morally blameworthy, any more so than if it had been any other disease, and certainly not in the eyes of the Tahitians, who saw nothing wrong in sexual promiscuity. In fact, the poisoning of the islanders with syphilis and the terrible consequences this had for them seem to fulfil a largely symbolic function in the *Supplément*. The real issue is, rather, the attitude of the French to sex, and specifically for the Vieillard the intensity of their sexual passions, contrasted with the simple, relaxed enjoyment of the Tahitians: 'tu es venu allumer en elles des fureurs inconnues. Elles sont devenues folles dans tes bras; tu es devenu féroce entre les leurs' (p.148).

I am tempted to think that Diderot is here indulging in a degree of sly boasting about what amounts to the remarkable sexual prowess of the French. But there is certainly no such ambivalence intended by the Vieillard (that is to say overtly by Diderot); the passions of the French, which consist in the overvaluing of sexual possession, thus represent both the pursuit of another 'bien imaginaire', and another aspect of the obsession with private property. This sexual possessiveness has the same kind of corrupting and destructive effect as material possessiveness: it creates previously unknown rivalry among the Tahitian women, and even leads the French to kill each other in competition for their favours. It is curious to note, in passing, that the Vieillard's evocation of the dangers of the passion of love is strangely reminiscent of Jansenism, though the Jansenists would scarcely have accepted as an ideal the uninhibited sexuality of the Tahitians, uncomplicated by moral taboos.

Thus far, indeed, one might well wonder what all this has to do with the sub-title of the work, 'sur l'inconvénient d'attacher des idées morales à certaines actions physiques qui n'en comportent pas'. But although the Vieillard does not make the point, except allusively by his reference to 'vertus chimériques', underlying the French attitude to sex as he describes it is the sexual morality of the Christian Church − which is graphically and comically (if unfairly) illustrated in the next stage of the work, the 'Entretien de l'Aumônier et d'Orou'.

Much of the effectiveness of this section is achieved by the use of the 'innocent eye' technique, as in Montesquieu's *Lettres persanes* or Voltaire's *Candide*, which here depends on Orou's total ignorance of religion, although this was another of Diderot's distortions: Bougainville had discovered that the Tahitians not only believed in a non-material deity, but were 'fort superstitieux', having priests who exercised over them 'la plus redoutable autorité' (*12*, p.257). Be that as it may, the technique requires the Aumônier to attempt to explain Christian morality to Orou in simple terms, and Diderot points the satire by ensuring that the explanation is (predictably) clumsy and ineffectual. The question of celibacy, in particular, is treated in a caricatural fashion: after the 'Mais ma religion, mais mon état' joke, the Aumônier can only answer 'Rien' when Orou asks him what monks actually do (p.175), and he confesses that he does not know why they are respected (p.176); he even readily admits that nuns 'sèchent de douleur, périssent d'ennui' (ibid.). Such views were, of course, Diderot's, as we know, for instance, from his *Encyclopédie* article 'Célibat' (*2*, VI, p.296) and from *La Religieuse*; but we must assume that Bougainville's real-life Aumônier would have done better than this in defending his calling.

If respect for celibacy is one aspect of Christian morality, however, it is the other side of the coin, Christian marriage, that Diderot is mainly interested in. Like the Vieillard's denunciation of colonialism and slavery, Orou's denunciation of European marriage initially represents it as constituting an utterly unjustifiable extension of the right of property over another 'être sentant, pensant et libre' (p.157). But this way of perceiving marriage is something of a side issue in the work, being used more as a debating point than for its own sake. The main emphasis is rather different: the question on which both Orou's criticism and the subsequent A-B discussion chiefly turn is the Christian insistence on constancy and fidelity in marriage, together with the associated taboo attached to sexual union outside it.

In his long speech beginning 'Ces préceptes singuliers [...]' (pp.157-59), much of which repeats what Diderot wrote in other works and in his letters, Orou argues that compulsory constancy and fidelity are 'contraires à la loi générale des êtres': to demand a constancy 'qui proscrit le changement qui est en nous', a fidelity 'qui borne la plus capricieuse des jouissances à un même individu', is to require a fixity in human beings which is belied not only by their own mortal flesh, but by the whole of nature, ever in a state of change and decay. In other words, Christian morality is completely unreasonable in that it is founded on an unreasonable view of human nature. A society based on such a morality is bound to have rules which are 'faits pour multiplier les crimes', demanding of men a kind of behaviour which is simply alien to them, and virtually encouraging them to become criminals.

The result is a state of moral and physical chaos, not to say anarchy. The attempt to enforce this topsy-turvy morality, whether by direct punishment or 'le blâme général' (p.159) directed against those who behave naturally, inevitably involves cruelty and injustice – and indeed worse: even the representative of Christianity in Diderot's argument cannot but accept as accurate the horrifying picture of depravity evoked by Orou as a necessary consequence, revealing European society as full of cheats, hypocrites and all kinds of criminals (p.160). From the point of view of the individual, these degrading anti-natural laws make men unhappy whether they obey them or, as happens more usually, disobey them. They are racked by internal contradictions, torn between the demands of nature and those of moral laws, either consumed with guilt for behaving naturally and breaking the law, or made even more deeply unhappy by the denial of their own natural instincts. From the point of view of society, the situation created is exactly that absence of *mœurs*, when the laws, good or bad, are not obeyed, which B later describes as 'la pire condition d'une société' (p.178).

What is more, such laws are not just pointlessly anti-natural, but positively anti-social. If, as Diderot and his contemporaries accepted, national prosperity usually increased with population size, then it made sense to do as the Tahitians did and regard each new child as an additional citizen, an addition to the effective wealth of the community. The stigma attached in Christian society to sexual intercourse, except in certain very restricted circumstances, together with the prestige accorded to celibacy, are incomprehensibly perverse in Orou's eyes, conflicting as they do with the material interests of the society as a whole. The story of Polly Baker, appearing before the court charged for the fifth time with having given birth to a child without being married, illustrates perfectly the nonsensical consequences of Christian morality. She has done no harm to anyone and is 'guilty' only of contributing to the good of the society in which she lives: 'Est-ce un crime d'augmenter les sujets de Sa Majesté dans une nouvelle contrée qui manque d'habitants?' (p.166). She is a victim of the depraved society described by Orou, which is not merely unjust, but inconsistent and hypocritical, condoning wickedness in men while punishing their innocent victims.

However, in all this demonstration that Christian morality concerning sex and marriage is quite nonsensical, a 'monstrueux tissu d'extravagances' (p.160), Diderot does not of course give Christianity a fair hearing, and the Aumônier is scarcely an adequate champion of his cause. He does, it is true, get to the

fundamental issue when he attempts to explain to Orou the
notion of Christian revelation, of a God who has decreed that
certain actions are good and others are bad (p.156). But he
subsequently seems to forget this crucial point and finds nothing
to say in response to Orou's rationalist challenge. The essence of
belief in a divine revelation is that it may well involve acceptance
of arbitrary moral principles — there would be little point in
God speaking to men to tell them only what they already knew
by natural means. For Orou, as for Polly Baker, who accuses
her judges of making laws 'qui changent la nature des actions et
en font des crimes' (p.166), actions are naturally and self-
evidently right or wrong. Priests and magistrates surely cannot
change that, he reasons: 'Peuvent-ils faire que ce qui est juste
soit injuste, et que ce qui est injuste soit juste?' (p.158). A more
resourceful Aumônier might have argued that it is only the
teaching of the Church, conveying and interpreting the will of
God, that can determine what is truly right or wrong.

At the heart of Christian morality lies the fall of man, the
belief that since that fall, man's nature is corrupt. Thus it is no
accident that Christian morality turns out to be anti-natural: it is
deliberately and consistently so. Orou thinks that he has made
unanswerable points when he tells the Aumônier that his
precepts are 'opposés à la nature', 'contraires à la raison' and
'contraires à la loi générale des êtres' (p.157); but the points are
quite without force for the believing Christian. The same is true
of his argument that the conflicting demands of religion and of
nature will inevitably pose terrible difficulties for man: it is *en
connaissance de cause* that the Church instructs man to repress
his natural instincts, and for the Christian, the triumph over the
temptations of nature is called 'virtue'.

It is precisely to virtues such as this that Diderot is referring
when the Vieillard dismisses the Europeans' 'vertus
chimériques': the rationalist arguments of his two rather
implausibly articulate Tahitians are diametrically opposed to the
Christian approach, inadequately represented as it is by the
implausibly inarticulate Aumônier. But the debate has already
gone, by implication, way beyond the mere question of sexual
morality. By rejecting the possibility of a morality based on

divine revelation and maintaining in general terms that nature provides a sound guide for human behaviour, Orou is in effect widening the discussion to include all aspects of morality.

Furthermore, I have until now deliberately simplified his argument: in fact, he evokes not just the clash between nature and religion, but the three-way conflict between nature, priests and magistrates – or, as B will later define it, between 'le code de la nature, le code civil, et le code religieux' (p.178) – a conflict which prevents man from being successfully any one thing, 'ni homme, ni citoyen, ni pieux' (p.158). The extra dimension, that of the 'code civil' and the 'citoyen', obviously linking up with Orou's notion of the general good (to which Polly Baker had so effectively contributed), is vitally important for understanding Diderot's approach to morality. He uses the indictment of Christian-European sexual morality as a starting point for a much wider discussion of the nature of morality in general, and for Diderot, certainly by this stage in his life, this was inseparable from a discussion of the organization of society.

6. Morality and the Organization of Society in Diderot's Thought

Not surprisingly, the *Supplément* was anticipated in many ways in Diderot's earlier works — he was, after all, nearly sixty when he wrote it — and it is easy to find plenty of instances in them where he had said much the same on the three topics I have discussed, his attitudes to sex, to nature and to contemporary French society. But on all these topics, while a consideration of parallels in other works may well throw more light on the evolution of his thought in general, it does not add a great deal to the comprehension of the *Supplément*. This is not true, however, of the discussion of the organization of Tahitian society and its moral and social implications for Europe. In this case, what Diderot has to say in the *Supplément* forms part of a debate which he conducted over a long period and in a variety of works, and it cannot be fully appreciated without situating it in the context of the evolving discussion to which it was an important contribution.

It is perhaps Diderot's loss of faith in God which provides the most appropriate starting point for an examination of his thought on morality. His earliest publication of any note was an *Essai sur le mérite et la vertu*, the translation of a work by Shaftesbury, but one in which a number of changes to the original text give a clear indication of Diderot's thinking at that time, showing him in 1745 to be an already sceptical deist. Within a few years, however, by the time he came to write the *Lettre sur les aveugles* in 1749, it is generally accepted that he had become an atheist.

Now although Diderot recognized, even in the *Essai*, that atheists *could* be virtuous, and indeed often were, it is clear from the beginning that he was bothered by the fact that, on the face of it, there was good reason to think that they probably would not be. Both in the *Essai* and in the *Pensées philosophiques* of 1746, he makes the traditional point that without the incentive of belief in God and the immortality of the soul, the atheist is less likely to be virtuous than the believer. It is, however, in the *Promenade du sceptique*, written in 1747, that this anxiety is given its most graphic expression. The work is a satirical, allegorical account of the three different paths men follow through life, the 'Allée des épines', the way of the Christians, the 'Allée des marronniers', the way of the philosophers, and the 'Allée des fleurs', the way of the seekers after worldly pleasures. All three are supposed to lead to 'le Prince', but it is far from certain that they do, especially in the case of the dangerous 'Allée des fleurs', which seems to be peopled mainly by refugees from the 'Allée des épines', enjoying the pleasures that are forbidden in their own path.

The 'Allée des fleurs' in fact offers an interesting prefiguration of the *Supplément*. Cléobule, the narrator, recounts how, on one of his visits there, he met a beautiful woman with whom he argued about the legitimacy of sexual pleasures. In response to his assertion that they are forbidden by 'the Prince', the lady retorts, like Orou, that such a wise ruler would surely not have given us instinctive needs and desires which he did not mean us to satisfy, and Cléobule ends up by conceding the argument and, like the Aumônier, by giving a good account of himself in practice: 'je lui présentai la main et la conduisis dans un cabinet de verdure, où je lui fis trouver ses raisons meilleures encore qu'elle ne les avait d'abord imaginées' (2, II, p.154).

But as far as the morality of the atheist is concerned, the crucial scene takes place in the 'Allée des marronniers'. Athéos, an atheist, returning home after a stroll with his philosophic friends, finds 'sa femme enlevée, ses enfants égorgés, et sa maison pillée'. Some time earlier, he had argued with one of the blindfolded Christians in the 'Allée des épines' to such good effect that the latter had abandoned his religious beliefs, and it is this renegade who is the presumed perpetrator of the crime: for had not Athéos taught him to 'mépriser la voix de la conscience et les lois de la société, toutes les fois qu'il pourrait s'en affranchir sans danger' (ibid., pp.138-39)?

Yet implicit in Diderot's anxiety about the moral dangers of atheism, is, of course, his own regard for virtue. Perhaps the renegade Christian was merely being 'conséquent', as Cléobule says (ibid., p.139), but there is no doubt that we are meant to be horrified by his wickedness, just as we are equally certainly meant to admire the virtue of the blind Saunderson in the *Lettre sur les aveugles*. Before proceeding further, therefore, it would no doubt be helpful to elucidate what Diderot understood by virtue.

Unfortunately, this is not easy to do, and for me, at any rate, his thinking on the subject is not always clear. From as early as the *Essai sur le mérite*, as Michèle Duchet has pointed out (*20*, pp.413 ff.), Diderot saw man as inherently sociable. Virtue consisted in behaving naturally; but for both Shaftesbury and Diderot, 'natural' and 'social' were usually interchangeable terms, so that behaving naturally meant contributing to the general good. Now this contribution to the general good referred initially to the biological process by which all living things naturally, even automatically, function in such a way as to contribute to the good of the whole of which they form part (see *2*, I, p.361). Starting from this organic view of the natural, it is easy to see how Diderot could argue that it was natural (and thus virtuous) for man to contribute to the good of the society to which he belonged – though the transition from the biological to the socio-political does not seem to me very convincing.

Be that as it may, although in the *Essai* Diderot had not yet become an atheist, it is clear that he no longer saw virtue in the absolute Christian sense, but rather as a contribution to the general good of society, so that its nature would vary with the nature of the society and according to circumstances. In the *Lettre sur les aveugles*, he goes further, and shows that our moral notions, far from being absolute, are dependent on the experience of our senses: the blind man he has questioned, for example, objects most strongly to theft, to which he is particularly vulnerable, but finds the obligation to clothe one part of the body rather than another quite incomprehensible. And turning to the question of sexual morality, Diderot speculates that in the land of the blind, either women would be communal, or the laws against adultery would be particularly severe.

This observation of the dependence of our moral attitudes on our physical experience helped to confirm Diderot's materialist, sensationalist view of man, according to which all our behaviour and indeed all our ideas are determined by our sense-experience, so that man cannot be considered as free. And if man's ideas and behaviour are determined in this way, his so-called intentions are irrelevant in a consideration of virtue: what matters is not intention, for which man is not responsible, but the actual end result, the contribution to the general good. In fact, Diderot reasoned, the very notions of virtue and vice become meaningless. As he wrote in 1756 in his well-known letter to the playwright Landois, which contains a vigorous résumé of his materialist philosophy and its moral implications, the terms 'vertu' and 'vice', implying a moral judgement, must be replaced by the descriptive words 'bienfaisance' and 'malfaisance' (*9*, I, p.214).

However, despite Diderot's demonstration that virtue had not merely no absolute meaning, but in fact no real meaning at all, at least not of the traditional Christian kind − and he was still making the same point about 'bienfaisance' and 'malfaisance' in the *Rêve de d'Alembert* (*4*, p.364), written in 1769 − he continued at the same time to write as if he still believed that man had an innate awareness of certain absolute moral qualities. In the *Entretien d'un père avec ses enfants*, the first version of which dates from 1771, one of the key themes is recognition of what Diderot calls 'l'équité naturelle', and he even affirms that 'la nature a fait les bonnes lois de toute éternité' (*4*, p.430). Some years earlier, Helvétius, in *De l'esprit* (1758), had denied the existence of absolute justice and injustice: he had been misled, Diderot claimed, by confining himself to the wide variety of forms taken by the just and unjust, instead of observing the nature of man. All he needed to do was to recognize that 'en quelque lieu du monde que ce soit, celui qui donne à boire à l'homme qui a soif, et à manger à celui qui a faim, est un homme de bien' (*1*, II, p.270).

But although Diderot appeared thus to affirm a belief in certain absolute moral values, and although he himself continued to express his fervent enthusiasm for virtue both in his works and in his correspondence, he was forced to recognize that not everyone shared it. As a convinced atheist, it is not surprising that he continued to be bothered by the apparent logic according to which he might have been as wicked as the renegade Christian of the *Promenade*. It was this problem posed by the existence of the logically wicked atheist that was to become the central theme of what is often considered his greatest literary achievement, *Le Neveu de Rameau*, the first draft of which was written probably in 1761 or 1762. To simplify a rather complex character, Rameau is an immoralist who sees it as only logical to seek one's own well-being, and whose sole object in life seems therefore to be the pursuit of happiness in its most obvious form, at least for the materialist, physical pleasure: 'boire de bon vin, se gorger de mets délicats, se rouler sur de jolies femmes, se reposer dans des lits bien mollets. Excepté cela, le reste n'est que vanité' (*6*, p.429).

Now obviously, Rameau, dedicated to the pursuit of self-interest, constitutes a social problem, and all the more so if, as he claims, it is he rather than 'Moi' who represents the norm. How can a society be organized to function in the interest of the general good if the majority of its members are like 'Lui'? But if 'Lui' presents a problem for society, his attitude is easy enough to understand. Indeed, 'Moi' actually shares his views about self-interest and the pursuit of happiness; but, unlike 'Lui', he happens to be virtuous, and thinks, what is more, that he and not Rameau is the norm, seeing the latter as a kind of moral freak. Of the two, it is, on the face of it, Rameau's position that is the more convincing, and the intellectual problem, as distinct from the social one, might thus seem to be rather: why should anyone be like 'Moi'? Why, in short, should an atheist be virtuous?

There was general agreement in the eighteenth century that happiness was the legitimate aim of man, and Diderot certainly shared this view: as he wrote in his *Mémoires pour Catherine II* in 1773, 'Il n'y a qu'un devoir, c'est d'être heureux' (*8*, p.235). It was no doubt an awareness of the potential social dangers of such views that led Diderot to cling to the idea, first enunciated in the *Essai sur le mérite*, that although it is legitimate for men to seek happiness, it can only come from virtue. And if this is the case, then to contribute to the good of society – to behave virtuously – must be to follow one's own self-interest.

But even in the *Essai*, where the idea is given its most emphatic formulation – 'point de bonheur sans vertu' – there is a strong element of wishful thinking about it. Diderot wanted to believe that true happiness necessarily depended on virtue, but life and history gave him all too much evidence that the wicked were not necessarily unhappy. In the year after the publication of the *Essai*, he tried to face up to the problem in the *Pensées philosophiques*, when reflecting specifically on the reasons an atheist might have for behaving virtuously: 'Sans la crainte du législateur, la pente du tempérament et la connnaissance des avantages actuels de la vertu, la probité de l'athée manquerait de fondement' (7, p.42). The key personal element distinguishing the good man from the bad man is clearly 'la pente du tempérament', though perhaps also the intelligence needed to recognize the 'avantages actuels de la vertu'. Nearly thirty years later, in 1774, Diderot was to give a very similar analysis of the problem in the *Entretien avec la Maréchale* (though this time omitting fear of the law, which he no doubt saw as self-evident). In answer to the Maréchale's question, 'Quel motif peut avoir un incrédule d'être bon, s'il n'est pas fou?', Diderot replies: 'Ne pensez-vous pas qu'on peut être si heureusement né, qu'on trouve un grand plaisir à faire le bien?[...] Qu'on peut avoir reçu une excellente éducation, qui fortifie le penchant naturel à la bienfaisance? [...] Et que, dans un âge plus avancé, l'expérience nous ait convaincus, qu'à tout prendre, il vaut mieux, pour son bonheur dans ce monde, être un honnête homme qu'un coquin?' (4, p.529). Again, the implication that not all men are like this is clear.

So to return to *Le Neveu de Rameau*, one of the few things that 'Moi' and 'Lui' agree about, as we have seen, is the pursuit of happiness; but 'Moi' sees no reason why this should lead to immorality. Although he too enjoys the pleasures of the senses, he vastly prefers – and this is surely Diderot speaking – the moral pleasures of *bienfaisance*. Now the reason for the difference is obviously 'la pente du tempérament'. Some people are 'heureusement nés', like the Diderot of the *Entretien avec la Maréchale*, whereas others are 'malheureusement nés', and the problem of how to convert the latter into constructive members of society has to be faced. Paradoxically, it is the anti-social Rameau who points the way towards the potential solution. For he is not deliberately anti-social, he does not seek deliberately to harm other people; he merely pursues his own material well-being, and this, as we have seen, Diderot recognized as both normal and legitimate. But since he also recognized that men's behaviour is determined by their environment, he realized that they are essentially modifiable and will respond to sticks and carrots. 'Lui' claims that his natural vices 'cadrent avec les mœurs de ma nation', and also that they are appreciated by his protectors (*6*, p.433); in other words, that society is so constructed that it is very much in his interest to behave 'wickedly'. The implication is clear, and it is made explicit by 'Lui' himself: 'Si par hasard la vertu avait conduit à la fortune, ou j'aurais été vertueux, ou j'aurais simulé la vertu comme un autre' (*6*, p.449). And of course, from the point of view of society, it matters little whether Rameau is really 'virtuous' or only pretending to be, so long as the result is *bienfaisance*.

It must be added that Diderot recognized that not all 'malheureusement nés' were as convertible as Rameau; there were others who were irremediably wicked, the true 'méchants', whom Diderot, through Rameau, exemplified maliciously in the enemies of the Encyclopedists, such as Palissot: men like that, he suggested, were naturally wicked in the same way as a tiger is naturally savage (*6*, p.455). But the true 'méchants' are few in number, and since nothing can be done about them (except, as Diderot proposed elsewhere, execution), their existence does not seriously affect the problem.

It may be that for 'Moi' and those like him, 'les avantages actuels de la vertu' are real enough, but it is clear that they are not so for the 'malheureusement nés'. What is needed, then, is a reform of the structure of society in which it will be in the interests of everybody, even the 'malheureusement nés', to contribute to the general good; in addition to the 'crainte du législateur', there must be positive incentives to *bienfaisance*. This is precisely the solution to the problem of social organization that Diderot sketched in his discussion with the Maréchale: 'faites que le bien des particuliers soit si étroitement lié avec le bien général, qu'un citoyen ne puisse presque pas nuire à la société sans se nuire à lui-même; assurez à la vertu sa récompense, comme vous avez assuré à la méchanceté son châtiment; [...] et ne comptez plus sur d'autres méchants que sur un petit nombre d'hommes, qu'une nature perverse que rien ne peut corriger entraîne au vice' (*4*, p.539). Tahiti as described by Orou is an imaginative exercise in constructing just such a society.

So much for the organization of the ideal society. But as far as the real world — that is to say France — was concerned, it might be argued that it was not 'Lui' but 'Moi' and the other 'heureusement nés' who had the potentially greater problem. The 'heureusement nés' were those who gained pleasure from *bienfaisance*, and when this was merely at the simple level of doing good to other individuals, there was no problem. But in a country with bad laws and corrupt moral standards, neither of which was really conducive to the general good — and there is ample evidence that this is how Diderot saw France — not only would a contribution to the general good often involve considerable personal disadvantage, but situations would be bound to arise when the only way to achieve it would be by breaking the rules.

The dilemma of the man of virtue confronted by the existence of bad laws was one Diderot was very conscious of — no doubt his own imprisonment at Vincennes for having written the *Lettre sur les aveugles* had focused his mind on it at that early stage in his career. In the *Salon de 1767*, he imagines a debate between two groups of philosophers, one of which, represented by Aristippus, defines virtue as 'l'habitude de conformer sa conduite à la loi', while the other, represented by Socrates, claims it is 'l'habitude de conformer sa conduite à l'utilité publique' (*1*, XI, p.121). The principal argument used by the conformists is that the freedom to challenge bad laws will inevitably lead to the disregard of even good ones, and the debate ends quite inconclusively. But the whole problem of the extent to which anyone is entitled to break the law continued to exercise Diderot's mind, and it was a few years later, in 1771, that he gave it rather fuller treatment in the *Entretien d'un père avec ses enfants*, significantly sub-titled *Du danger de se mettre au-dessus des lois*.

The *Entretien* consists of the discussion, mainly by 'Moi' (Diderot) and his father, of a series of cases in which the strict application of the law does not seem appropriate. Diderot himself consistently puts the heretical view, recommending that the law should be ignored, while his father, who is presented throughout as an admirable figure, is the conformist, pointing out the dangers implicit in his son's attitude. Once again, the debate is inconclusive, though it does seem to end with the father conceding some moral latitude and independence of action to the exceptionally wise individual like his son, who has claimed that 'à la rigueur il n'y a point de lois pour le sage': 'Je ne serais pas trop fâché [...] qu'il y eût dans la ville un ou deux citoyens comme toi; mais je n'y habiterais pas, s'ils pensaient tous de même' (*4*, p.443).

It was all very well to recognize, as Diderot did, that the moral laws of his own society were bad ones, and that Tahiti, at least as portrayed by Orou, offered a much more sensible form of social organization. But what was to be done about it, particularly in the light of the dangers, which he also recognized, inherent in breaking the law? This, as we shall see, is another of the important questions Diderot speculates about in the *Supplément*.

7. Orou's Solution: The Social Organization of Tahiti

Whatever Diderot's own attitude to virtue, he recognized, as we have seen, that some people were not naturally inclined to *bienfaisance*, and that these 'malheureusement nés' posed a major problem for the organization of society. When Orou explains to the Aumônier, however, what he considers to be the principles on which social morality should be based, he sees little problem: indeed, he does not even appear to recognize the existence of any 'malheureusement nés'.

Implicit in Orou's denunciation of the arbitrary and false values dictated by the Aumônier's magistrats and priests, seems to be a firm belief in the reality of absolute and permanent moral values, as we have seen: 'sont-ils maîtres du bien et du mal? Peuvent-ils faire que ce qui est juste soit injuste, et que ce qui est injuste soit juste?' (p.158). It soon becomes apparent, however, that he sees 'good' and 'bad' not in genuinely absolute terms, but as values related to the interests of society. It is true that he continues to speak as if he does see them as absolutes: 'Veux-tu savoir, en tout temps, et en tout lieu, ce qui est bon et mauvais?' (ibid.). But his explanation is rather disconcerting, making it clear that 'good' and 'bad' are dependent on things and circumstances: 'Attache-toi à la nature des choses et des actions; à tes rapports avec ton semblable; à l'influence de ta conduite sur ton utilité particulière et le bien général'.

It seems here that personal good and public good are merely the two factors to be taken into account, with no precedence being established. But as Orou goes on, public good emerges unequivocally as the first priority. Again he speaks in emphatically absolute terms: 'Tu es en délire, si tu crois qu'il y ait rien, soit en haut, soit en bas, dans l'univers, qui puisse ajouter ou retrancher aux lois de la nature' (pp.158-59). It is as if, despite having mocked the Aumônier's 'vieil ouvrier' and professing no understanding of the concept of a deity, Orou has somehow deified nature, whose eternal laws replace those of the Christian God. But what do these laws of nature amount to? 'Sa volonté éternelle est que le bien soit préféré au mal, et le bien général au bien particulier'. Although 'nature's' preference for good over evil seems to me little more than a matter of definition, the preference for the general over the individual is highly significant. To some extent, this must be understood in the light of Diderot's conviction that man is naturally a social animal, and that like other animals, his instincts lead him to work for the good of the species. But as I pointed out earlier, he tended to blur the distinction between the biological and socio-political senses of general good, and the context in which Orou here uses the term seems to indicate that it is meant in the latter sense. Nature wills the good of society as a whole − at the expense, it is implied, of the individual if that turns out to be necessary. So that good and bad, though absolute in one sense, are not really absolute terms at all, but designate first and foremost whatever is good and bad for society.

This, then, was presumably the sense in which Orou had been using the terms when he had argued earlier that priests and magistrates could not be 'maîtres du bien et du mal', as the somewhat less abstract continuation of his demonstration appears to confirm: 'Dépend-il d'eux d'attacher le bien à des actions nuisibles, et le mal à des actions innocentes ou utiles?' The point is made clearer by the examples he then gives: killing and stealing are 'actions nuisibles', harmful to other men and thus to the 'bien général'; and eating forbidden fruit (the biblical allusion is unmistakeable) or other kinds of food is an action which may not be 'utile' in the sense of contributing to the general good, but is obviously 'innocente' in that it does not harm it − and anyway certainly contributes to the good of the individual.

Orou's main point, of course, is to demonstrate that it is folly to attempt to replace these fixed notions by arbitrary ones: the result, as we saw in an earlier chapter, will be a world of topsy-turvy morality, a world in which 'il n'y a point de bonté qu'on ne pût t'interdire; point de méchanceté qu'on ne pût t'ordonner' (p.158). If the general good were no longer the object of the laws of society, men would be completely disorientated; they would be 'troublés dans l'état d'innocence', condemned without being guilty of an 'action nuisible', and 'tranquilles dans le forfait', because positively harmful actions would be officially permitted (p.159). They would in fact be neither 'hommes' nor 'citoyens', neither achieving personal happiness nor contributing to the good of society.

But the attempt to impose arbitrary, anti-natural rules is anyway doomed to failure, since nature cannot be overcome and the rules will be ignored: 'Tu ordonneras le contraire; mais tu ne seras pas obéi'; and this, as the Aumônier confesses, is what happens in France, despite the express orders of priests, magistrates and the 'vieil ouvrier'. The authorities in such a case are forced to choose between savage repression and allowing the laws to be broken, which is worse still for society: 's'ils ne sévissent pas, ce sont des imbéciles qui ont exposé au mépris leur autorité par une défense inutile' (p.159). And this, anticipating B's definition of 'la pire condition d'une société', was a point to which, as we have seen, Diderot attached considerable importance.

Yet at the centre of Orou's neat demonstration lie two over-simplifications, perhaps even confusions, giving the impression the Diderot was deliberately glossing over some inconvenient difficulties. To begin with, the assertion that 'bien' and 'mal' can be understood only in relative, social terms comes at the end of the argument, and though logically it ought to apply to what precedes, in practice the earlier point tends to be read differently. When Orou asks: 'sont-ils maîtres du bien et du mal?', and refers to the 'juste' and the 'injuste', we understand these terms as absolutes. And this interpretation seems to be confirmed by what follows: 'à ce compte, il n'y aurait ni vrai ni faux, ni bon ni mauvais, ni beau ni laid; du moins, que ce qu'il plairait à ton grand ouvrier, à tes magistrats, à tes prêtres, de prononcer tel'. When Diderot referred to this 'trinité', as Rameau calls it (6, p.467), of the 'vrai', the 'beau' and the 'bon', it was when he was thinking of moral goodness in absolute terms, analogous to and related to truth and beauty. Although killing and stealing *could* be seen as wrong because not in the interests of the general good, it seems to me that Orou and, through him, Diderot, were here quoting them as examples of behaviour which was intrinsically and in all circumstances bad. But in the case of killing at least, it is obvious that absolute good and the good of a particular society do not necessarily coincide, as Orou has here been implying: in other works, Diderot himself accepted without demur the need for both war and capital punishment.

But an even more crucial flaw in Orou's argument is his equation of – or perhaps confusion between – natural law and natural instinct. His long speech had begun, it will be remembered, as a response to the Aumônier's description of Christian sexual morality, with its insistence on constancy and fidelity, accompanied by ineffectual laws which were powerless to enforce them. Orou's principal argument was that these 'préceptes singuliers' will result in harm to the individual ('vous avez rendu la condition de l'homme pire que celle de l'animal'), and harm to society, in that they will not be obeyed ('Rien [...] te paraît-il plus insensé qu'un précepte qui proscrit le changement qui est en nous; qui commande une constance qui n'y peut être [...]?').

Now, up to a point, this fits in with Orou's later argument about the 'volonté éternelle' of nature. Although public good is to be preferred to private good, this does not rule out the satisfaction of private good, or 'utilité particulière', so long as this is not in conflict with the public good. Frequent changing of sexual partners may not contribute to the general good, but neither does it harm it, and so it is an 'action innocente', appropriately coming into the same category as eating forbidden fruit. But although Orou describes the rules imposing constancy and fidelity as 'contraires à la loi générale des êtres', it is clear that we are here concerned with a natural instinct, an urge to promote 'le bien particulier' which has nothing to do with 'le bien général', and it is because it is an instinct that it is foolish to try to control it. All 'la loi générale des êtres' seems to mean is 'the way people are'.

Yet the later argument seems to hinge on the so-called 'lois de la nature', which are expressed in the eternal will of nature, requiring not only that good should be preferred to bad, but that general good should be preferred to individual good. What precisely is meant by 'the will of nature' is far from clear, but since Orou continues 'tu ordonneras le contraire; mais tu ne seras pas obéi', we must assume that it is not just the expression of a moral imperative, a standard to which people feel they *ought* to conform, but something actually *within* people, dictating their actions. Even so, it seems unlikely that Orou, let alone Diderot, expects us to believe that men will refuse to prefer their own good to the general good when the two are in conflict; indeed, only two years later, Diderot was to describe as 'absurde' a system of government in which 'le citoyen est forcé continuellement de sacrifier son goût et son bonheur pour le bien de la société' (5, p.404). What I think he does mean here is that people will always naturally prefer the good to the bad (understood in a social sense), even when the law tries to make them behave otherwise.

The confusion becomes manifest, however, when Orou, moving from the general to the particular, asks the Aumônier whether in France people have sexual intercourse outside the officially permitted limits, and gets the expected answer. The reader might be forgiven for protesting that if people transgress the laws restricting sexual relations, it is because of a natural instinct, rather than from a desire to contribute to the good of society. In effect, Orou seems to equate 'the will of nature' with natural instinct, and one might well conclude that the very notion of the 'will of nature' is another red herring, just a way of referring to instinct in such a way as to legitimize it. The essence of his argument is really that, although instinct, the individual's urge to seek his own well-being, cannot be suppressed, this does not create a social problem since in fact there is, or at least there need be, no true opposition between general good and particular good.

Of course, if one sees procreation as the main aim of society, the argument is a tenable one. In the description of Tahiti that follows – and which is rather more effective than Orou's somewhat confused theoretical discussion of the principles of social organization – the source of all contributions to the general good is identified as an increase in population. The new-born child represents the very foundation of the true wealth of the society: 'ce sont des bras et des mains de plus dans Tahiti; nous voyons en lui un agriculteur, un pêcheur, un chasseur, un soldat, un époux, un père' (p.161). And since the desire to procreate is a universal natural instinct, there is no difficulty in harmonizing public good and private good in Tahiti.

Implicit in the whole concept of the need to link the two is the idea that, as Diderot argued elsewhere, self-interest is the dominant motivating force in human behaviour, and Orou explains that Tahitian society is indeed based precisely on this principle, contrasting it with the hypocritical 'fanfaronnade de vertu' of the French (p.173). It was in accordance with the principle of self-interest, and because of their permanent man-power shortage, he reveals, that the Tahitians had offered the French their women; there were not enough Tahitian males available to fecundate the more numerous women, and in any case, the French, whom the Tahitians recognized as more intelligent than they, were being used as a means of improving the stock (p.175). If it were not evident that this is all sheer fantasy on Diderot's part, and that this Tahiti is not, as it were, the same as the (more authentic) one in 'Les Adieux du Vieillard', Orou's claim that 'tout sauvages que nous sommes, nous savons aussi calculer' (ibid.) would make the Vieillard's reproaches to the French seem singularly hypocritical!

Once the natural urge to procreate has been satisfied, it is essential for children to be cherished and nurtured if their potential value for society is to be recognized. Following the principle of self-interest, Tahiti has its system of family allowances, which, incidentally, will also encourage anyone not instinctively so inclined to try to produce children. A woman's children are seen to be her dowry, for since a sixth of all the country's produce is allocated to the upkeep of children – and of the aged, a point I shall return to – 'plus la famille du Tahitien est nombreuse, plus elle est riche' (p.162). The implications are far-reaching. As Orou explains, it is not only the children who are cherished, but also, by the same token, mothers, and even potential mothers and fathers, all as a possible source of private wealth (pp.173-74). The implied contrast with French society − '*C'est ici* que les pleurs trempent [...]; *c'est ici* que les mères sont [...]; *c'est ici* qu'on prise [...]; *c'est ici* qu'on s'occupe [...]' (my italics) − is borne out by the Aumônier, who recognizes the effectiveness of self-interest rather than virtue when he admits that the French peasant is more concerned for his livestock than for his wife and children.

As for the restrictions on behaviour that the European sees as the most obvious manifestation of social organization, these are kept in Tahiti to an absolute minimum, for as the Aumônier reported, 'Rien n'y était mal par l'opinion ou par la loi, que ce qui était mal de sa nature' (p.177). That is to say that the only actions that were forbidden were those that were truly 'nuisibles', contrary to the general good. Since sexual intercourse does not come into this category, it is not hedged around with the kind of prohibitions that are customary in European society: Orou does not even understand the terms 'fornication', 'inceste' and 'adultère' (p.170).

Although, then, there is little need in Tahiti for restrictions, those that do exist, on the other hand, are effective, creating a society in which the laws are hardly ever disobeyed, in pointed contrast to France. Women wear white, grey or black veils as public indications of their unsuitability for sexual intercourse (no doubt a jocular allusion to nuns), and Orou claims initially that the only penalty for those who infringe the rules is public disapproval, 'le blâme' (p.169). A few pages later, however, he admits to the existence of more rigorous punishments − though the implication is that they are rarely needed − ranging from a reprimand for the parents of young men who abandon their chastity chains prematurely, to exile to the north of the island, or even slavery, for the 'vieilles dissolues', the sterile old women who cast aside their black veils to consort illicitly with men (pp.172-73). But the most appropriate and most effective deterrent, operating through self-interest, is perhaps the kind of fine imposed on the woman who does not wait the statutory month before changing sexual partners, and who must forfeit all right to any child whose paternity is thus in doubt; as a result, says Orou to the Aumônier, 'tu conçois que, parmi nous, les libertines sont rares, et que les jeunes garçons s'en éloignent' (p.168).

Orou's Tahiti thus seems remarkably like the recipe for the ideal society that Diderot outlined to the Maréchale (*4*, p.539, quoted earlier). The 'bien des particuliers' is indeed intimately linked to the 'bien général', in fact it is inseparable from it, and virtue — that is to say behaviour contributing to the general good — is indeed rewarded. There are even the small number of 'méchants', the 'libertines' made vicious by 'une nature perverse que rien ne peut corriger'.

Yet the treatment of the 'libertines' in Tahiti may well leave the modern reader feeling a little uneasy. The fate of sterile women, in particular, punished by deprivation, if nothing worse, because of a 'vice de naissance' or just old age, seems rather harsh — and contrasts oddly with what Diderot says in this work and elsewhere about the awful effects of enforced celibacy on nuns. Certainly here is a case where there is a clash between 'bien particulier' and 'bien général', and in conformity with the principles laid down by Orou, the 'bien général' is preferred. The prohibition can indeed be justified in terms of the general good, and if the wearers of black and grey veils are punished, it is precisely because they have sexual intercourse when 'il ne peut rien résulter de leur approche' (p.172); Diderot has taken care to have Orou point out that there is in fact a shortage of men, so that temporarily or permanently sterile women could be seen as using up valuable male seed unproductively.

Even so, if Diderot had chosen, their sexual activities could just as easily have been presented, by Orou's own principles, as 'actions innocentes' and thus morally neutral. One has the distinct feeling that sexual intercourse is justified in Diderot's version of Tahiti not on the grounds of pleasure, the legitimate gratification of the senses, but solely because it leads to procreation — a point which has been interestingly discussed in Adriana Sfragaro's article (*45*, especially p.1896). Even the Vieillard, it will be remembered, had depicted the Tahitians as glorying in sexual union because it represented 'le moment d'enrichir la nation et la famille d'un nouveau citoyen' (p.150). The quasi-religious ceremony of sexual initiation described by Orou (p.164) is no doubt meant to have a deliberate civic function, conferring prestige on a socially useful activity; at the same time, the effect of this cult of procreation is to suggest that sexual intercourse that is not productive is not justifiable. We seem to be very close to precisely the kind of morality that Diderot was setting out to challenge, as he indicated in the work's subtitle, the gratuitous repression of a harmless (if admittedly socially useless) activity – perhaps another unconscious reflection of his Christian background.

Tahitian society also seems to echo the Christian tradition in attaching the stigma of immorality to women, while tending to condone it in men – the very injustice that is so explicitly condemned by the story of Polly Baker. It is true that the man who lifts the grey or black veils and approaches the forbidden woman is designated a 'libertin' (p.169), but there is no mention of any punishment for him, apart from 'le blâme'. The injustice is even more blatant in the case of another category of *libertinage*: whereas the woman who changes partners before the month is up is seen as a 'libertine' and duly punished, her partners seem to be regarded as innocent, and one of them will actually be rewarded by receiving the child conceived at the time. And although rape, 'la violence d'un homme', is seen in principle as 'une faute grave', it seems in practice to be tolerated, since 'il faut une plainte publique, et il est presque inouï qu'une fille ou qu'une femme se soit plainte' (p.173).

But perhaps the women do not complain because after all, if a child is the result, the general order will have benefited and their own wealth increased. In Orou's picture of Tahiti, Diderot has attempted to visualize a society in which morality is entirely dependent on the general good, but he has allowed many ambiguities to survive. The question of violence against the individual is rather glossed over, and if rape is theoretically a crime, it is perhaps because, like killing, it is bad in absolute terms, regardless of its implications for the general good. In the same way, if one sixth of the country's produce is allocated to the upkeep of the aged as well as of children, it is no doubt because Diderot (aged nearly sixty!) saw respect for the elderly as absolutely desirable, whether or not it contributed to the good of society.

There are similar inconsistencies in his attempt to show that aesthetic as well as moral ideas are variable and socially determined. The Aumônier comments on the difference between two contrasted ideals of feminine beauty, related in Europe to '[le] plaisir d'un moment', and in Tahiti to 'une utilité plus constante' (p.164). But when Orou asks the Aumônier if he has ever seen 'autant de beaux hommes et autant de belles femmes que dans Tahiti' (p.169), it is a fixed, universal (though no doubt European) notion of beauty that is implied. The picture is further complicated by the alleged remark of one Tahitian woman to another: 'Tu es belle, mais tu fais de laids enfants; je suis laide, mais je fais de beaux enfants, et c'est moi que les hommes préfèrent' (p.165). This too suggests an absolute rather than a socially dependent notion of beauty, though here Diderot seems to have sacrificed consistency of detail for the sake of the epigrammatic and paradoxical formulation, the effect of which may well more than compensate for the sacrifice.

To a great extent, this concern for rhetorical effect rather than consistency is in keeping with Diderot's whole approach to the presentation of Tahitian society. He was not, I think, too worried about inconsistencies of detail in what was essentially a provocative and often light-hearted sketch of a kind of anti-Europe, and I do not believe that he expected his reader to take the fantasy world of Tahiti that emerges from the conversation of Orou and the Aumônier as a serious utopian ideal. Diderot delighted in using the dialogue form as a method of examining attractive hypotheses, and the way the work is structured invites us to join with A and B as they look at Orou's solution to the problem of social organization and comment on its implications.

8. A and B: the Lessons of Tahiti

Diderot's presentation of Tahiti as an 'anti-Europe', however fanciful, is obviously intended to provoke speculation about the implications it might have for European society, and it is the examination of these implications that is the purpose of the final dialogue between A and B. To begin with, they both seem to agree with the principles of social organization laid down by Orou, and to confirm the truth of his assumptions about what is wrong with European society. The picture of man torn between priests, magistrates and nature is echoed by B's three 'codes', 'le code de la nature, le code civil, et le code religieux', which make contradictory demands on man, placing him in an impossible position, 'd'où il est arrivé qu'il n'y a eu dans aucune contrée, comme Orou l'a deviné de la nôtre, ni homme, ni citoyen, ni religieux' (p.178). And this was an argument that Diderot was attached to, using it repeatedly in various texts written both before and after the *Supplément*; indeed, the passages in which it figures are so numerous that, in the words of Michèle Duchet, 'leur nombre même impose l'idée comme une idée-force' (*20*, p.440).

Orou's solution to this conflict had been a simple one: laws should not attempt to run counter to nature, because, among other things, people would simply not obey them. He had likened the authorities trying to enforce repressive laws to 'des bêtes féroces qui battent la nature' (p.159), and B declares similarly: 'vous deviendrez féroces, et vous ne réussirez point à me dénaturer' (p.183). The obvious conclusion would seem to be that the 'code civil' should therefore be based on the 'code de la nature', and A and B appear to agree that 'la loi civile ne doit être que l'énonciation de la loi de nature' (p.178). B even maintains that it is only in Tahiti that the condition of man is a happy one (p.185), no doubt because, as he had said earlier, 'le

Tahitien [...] s'en est tenu scrupuleusement à la loi de nature' (p.178).

All this might well lead the reader to assume that Diderot was building up to a clear preference for Tahiti over France, for the 'natural' over the civilized, and consequently to an argument in favour of rejecting society's nonsensical laws and social conventions. And this, I believe, is exactly what Diderot wants him to assume; but only in order to be able to correct him. Throughout the discussion, A, who in some measure represents the reader, articulates, usually in question form, the various assumptions that seem to have been suggested, and each time, B either tells him he is wrong, or gives a pointedly evasive and equivocal reply. Diderot's polemical technique consists of saying to the reader: 'What you have read so far will no doubt have led you to certain apparently obvious conclusions; but the conclusions are in reality far from obvious, and the problem is not as simple as you think.' The technique is neatly embodied in the discussion about what is and is not natural: A assumes from what B has said that he believes that coquetry and jealousy are not 'dans la nature', but when he seeks confirmation of this, B puts him down with: 'Je ne dis pas cela' (p.179-80).

Although B refers, like Orou, to the law of nature, he clearly means something very different by it. Nature is no longer seen as a quasi-divine power, willing men to prefer good to bad and general good to particular good. It is true that B agrees with A that the 'loi civile' should be based on the 'loi de nature'; but what does he mean by 'la loi de nature'? When A, encouraged by B's agreement, refers to it as being 'gravée au fond de nos cœurs' (p.178), B is quick to correct him. In common with the other radical thinkers of his time, Diderot rejected Descartes's doctrine of innate ideas, and this is what B does, giving a standard eighteenth-century materialist picture of man: 'Nous n'apportons en naissant qu'une similitude d'organisation avec d'autres êtres, les mêmes besoins, de l'attrait vers les mêmes plaisirs, une aversion commune pour les mêmes peines: ce qui constitue l'homme ce qu'il est' (ibid.). This is the way people are — Orou's 'loi générale des êtres' — a collection of instinctive likes and dislikes which it is impossible to change. It is a waste of time to tell man not to eat forbidden fruit, and not to indulge in certain categories of sexual relationship, so-called adultery and incest for example, for 'l'empire de la nature ne peut être détruit' (p.182).

Thus far, it might seem that despite the difference of opinion about the law of nature, B's approach to morality has turned out to be much the same as Orou's. In fact, there are important divergences. In keeping with Diderot's empirical approach to thinking, it is the perception of man as he is, claims B, that must serve as a basis for 'la morale qui lui convient' (p.178). But although Diderot was, broadly speaking, a materialist, he was quick to reject an over-simplified application of materialism, as his detailed refutation of Helvétius's *De l'homme*, some two years after the *Supplément*, amply illustrates. Man may be, at bottom, an *ensemble* of instinctive inclinations and aversions, but the *ensemble* is an extremely complex one, and all the more so in modern, socialized man.

In any case, Diderot makes it clear that to say that moral laws should be based on man as he actually is, does not necessarily mean, as Orou implies, that they should coincide with natural urges, and this is so merely from the point of view of personal happiness, let alone that of the needs of society. The solution to the problem of sexual morality is by no means as simple as the example of Tahiti appears to suggest. Certainly, A and B do not dissent from Orou's criticisms of European rules concerning constancy and fidelity; and initially, at any rate, nostalgia for a simple and uninhibited approach to sex seems to be implied in B's irritation ('Ne vous fâchez pas', says A) and impatience with the 'préliminaires de convention' which 'consument la moitié de la vie d'un homme de génie', contrasted with the attractive directness of sexual exchanges in Tahiti: 'Le Tahitien nous dirait: [...] Homme, présente-toi franchement si tu plais. Femme, si cet homme te convient, reçois-le avec la même franchise' (pp.180-81). But immediately afterwards, B's own analysis of the psychology of sexual relationships, especially from the point of view of the woman, drastically modifies this impression. This kind of sexual freedom, he admits, is conceivable only in the truly primitive state of nature, which he describes significantly as 'triste et sauvage', and in which 'deux êtres libres, jeunes et parfaitement innocents', yielding to their natural impulses, would end up 'tristes tous deux' (p.181). So that the apparently artificial courtship rituals of European man have a sound basis in human experience and are quite properly embodied in moral laws. It is thus that 'on a consacré la résistance de la femme', and that 'la violence de l'homme', taken lightly in Tahiti, 'devient un crime dans nos cités' (p.182).

Basing moral laws on what is natural in man is therefore made all the harder because of the difficulty of knowing precisely what is or is not natural. It would seem that 'la résistance de la femme' is, indirectly, natural, and so, A and B agree, is 'la galanterie' (p.179). But what of the more unpleasant aspects of sexual relationships? Diderot had initially written as if he believed that coquetry and jealousy, like constancy and fidelity, were not natural. In the early version of the *Supplément* published by Dieckmann, A interpreted B's analysis of coquetry as meaning that it was not 'dans la nature', and B did not demur; and a few lines later, B's explanation of jealousy, 'conséquence de nos fausses mœurs, et d'un droit de propriété étendu sur un objet sentant, pensant, voulant et libre' (*11*, p.55), clearly implied that it too was not natural. But on revising his text, Diderot seems to have had second thoughts about what was natural. A's assumption about B's view of coquetry was turned into a question, to which B now replied: 'Je ne dis pas cela'; and the explanation of jealousy was enlarged and transformed by the crucial addition of 'Passion d'un animal indigent et avare qui craint de manquer' (p.180). A seems to miss the significance of this, enabling Diderot to drive home his new point in the revised version by neatly using exactly the same question-answer formula as he had with coquetry: '*A*. Ainsi la jalousie, selon vous, n'est pas dans la nature? - *B*. Je ne dis pas cela'.

The modification of this passage has in effect introduced an important new point into the argument. It is true that, in the earlier version of the text, in addition to the general ambiguity of the picture of nature, Diderot had intimated that even without the intervention of civilization and laws, natural man could be led to 'la dépravation' as well as to 'la lumière' (p.184). But here, in the revised version, the principle is explicitly formulated for the first time: 'Vices et vertus, tout est également dans la nature'.

Natural instincts, then, are not necessarily good, even though B continually *seems* to be saying the contrary. Having apparently equated nature and happiness in his misleading cry of 'combien nous sommes loin de la nature et du bonheur!' (p.182), he goes on to identify the origin of the unhappiness of European man as residing in the conflict between natural man and the 'homme artificiel' that has been created within him. The very choice of the pejorative term 'artificiel' suggests approval for natural man; yet in the continuation of the same passage, B refers to 'l'homme moral et artificiel', thereby implying an almost Freudian distinction between instinctive amoral man and socialized moral man which recognizes the superiority of the latter.

So that if laws must take account of natural instincts – and this is clearly only selectively desirable – the justification for it has to be solely on the grounds of expediency. Not only do anti-natural laws make men unhappy, but they will provoke them to disobedience, and on this score, B is categorical, defining 'mœurs' – which here seems to mean 'virtue' – as 'une soumission générale et une conduite conséquente à des lois bonnes ou mauvaises' (p.178). This is indeed rather like the definition of 'vertu' given by the conformist group of philosophers in the *Salon de 1767* (quoted earlier), but it is noticeable that B goes farther by introducing the explicit principle that even bad laws should be obeyed, a point which he stresses by claiming that when the laws, good or bad, are not obeyed, it is the worst of all situations, for there are no *mœurs* at all.

The result would seem to be an impasse even if the laws are good: if 'vices et vertus, tout est également dans la nature', even good laws are bound to be repressive, and men, or some of them, are bound to be unhappy. But Diderot's discussion makes it very clear that he thinks that, in France at any rate, most laws are bad, which creates an even worse impasse: either they are obeyed, and men are made unhappy; or they are disobeyed, and it is 'la pire condition d'une société'.

Once again, the argument seems to have led to a firm preference for the primitive over the civilized, and when A returns to his questioning to ask if this is indeed what B thinks, B replies that it is only in Tahiti that man is happy, just as earlier he had declared that 'excepté dans ce recoin écarté de notre globe, il n'y a point eu de mœurs' (p.178). But it is clear by now that Tahiti offers no solution, and Diderot is using it manifestly as an unattainable ideal, rather like Eldorado in Voltaire's *Candide*, in which the pessimistic philosopher Martin lamented that 'il y avait peu de vertu et peu de bonheur sur la terre; excepté peut-être dans Eldorado, où personne ne pouvait aller' (*16*, p.200). Rousseau too had maintained in his *Discours sur l'inégalité* that once civilization had progressed beyond a critical point, there was no possibility of going back to the primitive 'golden age' society he had held up as an ideal. Civilized modern man has progressed too far to be able to return to the simple life of Tahiti.

As for the true state of nature, it is not even tempting, no matter how bad modern society may be. Apart from anything else, the average life span of civilized man is longer than that of 'l'homme sauvage' (p.185). Diderot here passes over the point rather rapidly, and even, perhaps, half dissociates himself from it by attributing it to A, and by giving to B a somewhat enigmatic response; but it is relevant to notice that, two years later, in his refutation of *De l'homme*, he saw it as absolutely conclusive: 'La durée moyenne de la vie de l'homme policé excède la durée moyenne de la vie de l'homme sauvage. Tout est dit' (*1*, II, p.411). And in the same text − perhaps recalling Bougainville's Pécherais − he was to make his preference for civilization even more emphatic: 'j'aime mieux le vice raffiné sous un habit de soie que la stupidité féroce sous une peau de bête. J'aime mieux la volupté entre les lambris dorés et sur la mollesse des coussins d'un palais, que la misère pâle, sale et hideuse étendue sur la terre humide et malsaine et recélée avec la frayeur dans le fond d'un antre sauvage' (ibid., pp.411-12).

If, then, a civilized society is to be preferred, it must be one in which the laws, even if they are bad, are obeyed. And this, I think, is what leads Diderot to propose as a second best to Tahiti the ferociously tyrannical government of Venice. Of course, as A's surprise perhaps indicates, Diderot did not seriously approve of what he elsewhere described as 'l'atrocité des lois' of Venice (*1*, VI, p.447); there is obviously a strong element of provocative perverseness here, which is indeed characteristic of his way of jolting his readers by unexpected challenges to their assumptions. Nevertheless, Venice does (allegedly) illustrate B's hypothesis of a society in which bad laws are obeyed: the result may be 'mauvaises mœurs', but that is better than no *mœurs* at all. The paradoxical effect of the repressive laws is in fact a form of 'abrutissement' (p.185), analogous to what A calls 'l'état de nature brute et sauvage' (p.184).

Now A's questioning up to this point has, in a sense, posed an entirely theoretical problem, with no practical implications for already civilized man: 'faut-il civiliser l'homme, ou l'abandonner à son instinct?' (p.183). But after the remarks about Venice, he formulates the question in a different way, at last making explicit the dilemma which I believe Diderot has had in mind throughout the A-B discussion of Tahiti: 'reviendrons-nous à la nature? nous soumettrons-nous aux lois?' (p.186). Given B's definition of *mœurs*, reinforced by the example of Venice, a conformist reply to the final question might seem now to be inevitable. Yet just before the introduction of Venice into the argument, B had launched into what looked to A like praise for the anarchy of Calabria. B appears to see the Calabrians as *de facto* savages, living in a state of 'barbarie', which, for all 'l'atrocité de quelques grands crimes', was responsible for far less human destruction than civilized societies (p.184). Diderot does not, I think, intend us to see Calabria as a society in which the laws are broken: it is presented rather as a country in which the rule of law has simply not been accepted. And rightly not accepted, it is implied, for the denunciation of the existing laws of civilized societies is unambiguous. The so-called 'sages législateurs' are nothing better than 'une poignée de fripons', and the implication is not merely that all actual societies are and have been governed by bad laws, but that good laws are scarcely conceivable: 'Méfiez-vous de celui qui veut mettre de l'ordre.

Ordonner, c'est toujours se rendre le maître des autres en les gênant' (ibid.).

After this, it seems reasonable enough for A to ask: 'Ainsi vous préféreriez l'état de nature brute et sauvage?', and B's reply, 'Ma foi, je n'oserais prononcer', may well appear somewhat surprising. It does seem that this section of the dialogue, with its apparent praise of anarchy, has tended to cloud still further an already confusing argument. Yet it is important to realize that this was quite intentional on Diderot's part: we discover from Dieckmann's edition that the whole passage (from 'Méfiez-vous de celui' to 'qu'en concluez-vous?', pp.184-85) was missing from the earlier manuscript. In other words, Diderot did not make the revision of his text an opportunity for simplifying and polishing the argument in order to lead as neatly and as compellingly as possible to his conformist conclusion; he was less concerned with producing a watertight demonstration than with giving an honest account of the problem, and so introduced complexity and even confusion into the discussion, just as he had done by making the addition about vice and virtue being equally natural. The result is a very deliberate oscillation in the line of the argument, which disconcerts the reader as effectively as it is intended to. If Diderot keeps us guessing throughout the 'Suite du dialogue entre A et B', it is not, I think, primarily as an artistic device (though it is this too), but rather as a reflection of his own complex response to an intractable problem.

When A finally asks: 'nous soumettrons-nous aux lois?', B for once is not evasive and opts unequivocally for unqualified obedience to the law. But the argument up to this moment could easily have gone either way, and B's disappointingly tame conclusion does not appear to follow at all logically from a challenging debate in which pros and cons were pretty evenly balanced. In fact, the main justification he advances for his conclusion is a completely new point, though it is one that Diderot had previously made in the *Neveu de Rameau*, the *Salon de 1767* and the *Entretien d'un père*, namely that the breaking of bad laws can lead to the breaking of good ones; indeed, B repeats almost textually the words of Aristippus in the *Salon*: 'je me soumettrai à la loi, de peur qu'en discutant, de mon autorité privée, les mauvaises lois, je n'encourage par mon exemple la multitude insensée à discuter les bonnes' (*I*, XI, p.123).

But the Aristippus-Socrates debate, it will be remembered, like the one in the *Entretien d'un père*, had been inconclusive. Whereas here, by giving Aristippus's argument to B, and by making it the conclusion of the work, Diderot seems to have taken sides in the debate. However, if the logic of the debate itself does not appear to lead to the firm preference for conformism which concludes it, we should perhaps look elsewhere for the decisive factors which led him to break the logical stalemate.

The clue is to be found, I believe, in the social pragmatism of B's concluding speech: let us protest that 'la honte, le châtiment et l'ignominie' have been unjustly attached to certain innocent actions, but 'ne les commettons pas, parce que la honte, le châtiment et l'ignominie sont les plus grands de tous les maux' – recalling 'le blâme' which Orou claimed was so effective in Tahiti. Diderot was here surely speaking from personal experience. To begin with, ever since his imprisonment in 1749, he had indeed chosen conformity to the law as the wisest course, and the very fact that the *Supplément*, like virtually all his most challenging works, was not published in his lifetime, bears witness to this. But more specifically, and this was something particularly affecting the very aspects of conventional sexual morality he was attacking in the *Supplément*, there was the question of his beloved daughter Angélique.

A few days after her marriage in September 1772, Diderot wrote her a deeply earnest letter, full of pressing advice as to her future behaviour. Exactly at the time when he must have been working on the *Supplément*, he urged her to conform absolutely and in every detail to the moral conventions of their society, especially those regarding fidelity and constancy, both for the sake of her own happiness, and indeed for the sake of his. He even warns her against indiscreet displays of affection for her husband which might lead her to be suspected, however wrongly, of immorality; it is not enough to *be* virtuous, what is important above all (for a woman at least) is to enjoy the public esteem accorded to the appearance of virtue: 'C'est un grand malheur que de perdre la considération attachée à la pratique de la vertu, et que d'être confondue par l'opinion fausse qu'on donne de soi, dans la foule de celles auxquelles on a la conscience de ne pas ressembler. On se révolte contre cette injustice, et l'on a tort. On a le droit de juger les femmes sur les apparences' (*8*, XII, p.125). Small wonder, we may think, that the *Supplément* concludes with an exhortation to imitate the Aumônier, 'moine en France, sauvage dans Tahiti'.

9. Postscript: the Significance of the Supplément

The apparent discontinuity between the debate embodied in the *Supplément* and its conclusions poses in a particularly acute form the question of just how seriously we should take the work, and what meaning, if any, we should read into it. To some extent, this is always a problem with Diderot: his thought is almost invariably expressed in the form of debate rather than as demonstration followed by conclusion, and it is probably safe to say that no one of his philosophical works presents a single unequivocal view on any one subject. They virtually all have the same approach: the examination of tempting hypotheses, usually by means of dialogues, which enable the author to appear to observe almost as a spectator the discussion of ideas to which he feels attracted but not necessarily committed. The creation of the different levels of dialogue in the *Supplément* is, as we have seen, particularly effective in achieving this kind of distancing of the author from the ideas he is holding up for inspection. The aim is to point the way not to a conclusion, but to an awareness of the complexity of the problems under discussion, an aim which is further served by Diderot's favourite strategy of teasing and provoking the reader, leading him to make assumptions about the direction of the debate and the author's meaning, which are thereupon shown to be quite wrong.

Needless to say, all of this makes it hazardous to look for simple conclusions about the meaning of any of his works, and this is particularly true of the *Supplément*. Nevertheless, it may be useful to resume some of the principal points that emerge from the debate that we have been examining, and to look at them briefly in the context of Diderot's thought in the years that followed.

At the most obvious level of the *Supplément*, the discussion of sexual mores, there is certainly no ambiguity about the condemnation of European-Christian conventions. Nor, ultimately, is there any about the practical conclusions Diderot suggests we should draw from this condemnation, which does not in any way contradict the policy of social conformity advocated at the end, any more than it does his advice to his daughter. Even in Tahiti, according to Orou, 'le blâme' operated as an effective deterrent to prevent people from breaking the rules, and B, surely here the voice of Diderot, sees public disgrace as the worst of all evils; happiness is therefore dependent on bowing to the conventions of one's own society, however unreasonable they may be.

But the principal interest of the *Supplément* lies in its political implications, and again there is no ambiguity about the central point: since behaving naturally (procreating) contributes to the general good, then it should be encouraged instead of being restricted, and there need be no conflict between the interest of the individual and the interest of society. Now to the modern reader, accustomed to Malthusian anxieties about over-population, the flaw in the argument is obvious; but Diderot seems to have believed like his contemporaries (wrongly) that the population of France was declining, and that increase in population normally led to an increase in prosperity. He does, it is true, envisage in the Ile des Lanciers (nowadays called Akiaki) a society in which space and resources are strictly limited and population control has to be practised: but he clearly sees this as a freak, and does not stop to reflect on the difficulties there would be in such a society of reconciling private and public good.

In any case, although sexual behaviour appears to be intended by Diderot to be seen as illustrative, the principle of solving the problem of social organization by allowing people to give free rein to their natural impulses in the knowledge that this will contribute to the general good, cannot easily be extended beyond the example of procreation. Perhaps in the end the only general principle of social organization that emerges from the work is the rather vague one of providing incentives for virtue (defined as contribution to the general good), in addition to the more usual punishments for anti-social behaviour.

However, the main political interest of the *Supplément* lies, I think, elsewhere, not so much in what one may call its utopianism, as in the practical implications of its unequivocal condemnation of French society. The dilemma evoked is the one which was embodied in A's final question to B, and which, as we have seen, was a recurrent theme in Diderot's thought: 'nous soumettrons-nous aux lois?'.

Despite B's unambiguously conformist answer, reinforcing his earlier declaration that even bad laws should be obeyed, the *Supplément* provides an excellent illustration of the Socrates-Aristippus tension which existed at the heart of Diderot's political thought, and which, particularly during the last years of his life, was pulling it continually in two diametrically opposed directions. On the one hand, certainly, there was the conformism of Diderot's father in the *Entretien d'un père*, according to which obedience to the law was supremely desirable, as much for the peace of mind of the individual as for the health of the body politic – and this, I think, can be seen as the dominant theme. But, at the same time, there was the 'Moi' of the *Entretien d'un père*, whose assertion of the right of the wise man to break bad laws reflected an anarchistic tendency in Diderot which sometimes, at the extreme, revealed itself in a dislike of all authority; the 'Méfiez-vous de celui qui veut mettre de l'ordre' of the *Supplément* was frequently an underlying theme in his works of this period, and was echoed, in particular, in more than one passage of his contributions to the *Histoire des deux Indes*.

Now this was no mere hypothetical dilemma for Diderot: as, in his latter years, he became increasingly a respected pillar of the community, even a friend of those in power, the problem of his own conduct in a society which he saw as badly governed and corrupt, perhaps irredeemably so, presented itself to him with particular force. It is important, however, not to overlook the fact that the conformist conclusion of the *Supplément* was also an unmistakably reformist one, as well as being an emphatic call to protest: 'Nous parlerons contre les lois insensées jusqu'à ce qu'on les réforme [...] *crions incessamment* qu'on a attaché la honte, le châtiment et l'ignominie à des actions innocentes' (my italics). This very much reflects what Diderot saw as the role of the philosopher – in other words his own role – in society. 'Le philosophe [...] éclaire les hommes sur leurs droits inaliénables', he declared to Catherine II (*8*, p.235), and the same vision of the philosopher, described as the 'défenseur des droits de l'humanité' (*1*, III, p.24), was to be one of the key themes of the *Essai sur les règnes de Claude et de Néron*.

A few months after writing the *Supplément*, Diderot set off on his journey to Russia to visit Catherine II in St Petersburg, and his conversations with the Czarina seemed to afford him a unique opportunity to put into practice his views about the mission of the philosopher. However, if on a personal level he certainly admired Catherine greatly, it seems likely that after his initial hopes, he soon realized that his enthusiastic advocacy of drastic political reform (subsequently written up in the *Mémoires pour Catherine II*) was falling on deaf ears; and contemporary evidence indeed confirms that Catherine saw Diderot's projects as wildly impracticable. It seems to have been only on his return from Russia that he read her own proposals for reform, and his demonstration of their inadequacy in his *Observations sur le Nakaz* makes it clear that his disillusionment was complete.

Although he expressed the view in the *Mémoires pour Catherine II* that bad laws could not last, it became increasingly apparent that he despaired of ever changing them by reform, particularly in the *Observations sur le Nakaz* and in the *Histoire des deux Indes*; as Yves Benot has shown (*28*, especially pp.219-20, 239-40), open justifications of revolution occur throughout Diderot's contributions to the latter. In his correspondence as much as in these works, there are repeated indications that he saw France as beyond all hope of reform, and his view of the only remedy left was made graphically clear in a striking image which he used three times, first in 1771, even before the *Supplément*, in a letter to John Wilkes, and subsequently in the *Réfutation d'Helvétius* and the *Histoire des deux Indes*: 'On me demandait un jour comment on rendait la vigueur à une nation qui l'avait perdue. Je répondis: comme Médée rendit la jeunesse à son père, en le dépeçant et en le faisant bouillir' (letter to Wilkes, *9*, XI, p.223). And in 1778, he saw the revolt of Britain's American colonies, which he greeted with enthusiasm, as a dire warning for other governments (*1*, III, p.324).

But if Diderot accepted the need for revolution, it was only on the condition that the bad order, or lack of order, that was destroyed should be replaced by a new and good order: the fear of anarchy and of the 'multitude insensée' evoked by Aristippus in the *Salon de 1767* remained very much alive in his mind. In the *Observations sur le Nakaz* (*5*, p.372), he reiterated exactly the definition of *mœurs* that B had given in the *Supplément*, and this, the necessity of obeying even bad laws, was the view to which he most consistently returned. The very work into which Diderot inserted his eulogy of the American revolution, the *Essai sur les règnes de Claude et de Néron*, had as its main theme a sustained defence of the philosopher Seneca's co-operation with the wicked Nero, mainly on the grounds that he was thus able to do far more good than if he had attempted to defy the tyrant. The element of self-justification in the work is obvious. Diderot saw himself as taking the only reasonable course of action, the one advocated at the end of the *Supplément*, that of protesting against unjust laws while continuing to observe them. It was in the *Essai* that he was most eloquent about the social responsibility of the philosopher, whose duty he saw as being to protest against injustice, even at the risk of persecution and perhaps death.

By not publishing his more daring works, Diderot tried to stay out of trouble (and mostly succeeded); but he had by no means opted out of the struggle. Many of his most radical works were circulated throughout Europe in Grimm's *Correspondance littéraire*, and, at the same time, he was preparing a second edition of the *Encyclopédie*. In addition, recent research has shown that he made very substantial contributions to Raynal's *Histoire des deux Indes*, which were at least as outspoken as anything he had written under his own name. It has further been suggested that any assessment of Diderot's contribution to the general movement of intellectual protest should take account of the works published by his friends, especially d'Holbach, on whom he had a very great influence (see *28*, p.43).

It is in this context that the *Supplément* has to be seen. Although it was not published until after Diderot's death, it did circulate in the *Correspondance littéraire* and was known to his friends, and it should perhaps be seen, as much as anything, as the kind of powerful discussion piece which played such an important part in creating the general ferment of ideas which went on around him. Like so many of his works, it threw off ideas like a catherine-wheel, and certainly raised more questions than it answered. Diderot never did offer satisfactory solutions to the problems he posed in the *Supplément*; but the discussion of these problems, which made a by no means insignificant contribution to his philosophical and political thought, remains, even for the modern reader, challenging and thought-provoking.

Select Bibliography

A great many of Diderot's works remained unpublished during his lifetime, and the process of tracing his manuscripts and establishing texts has been long and complicated. New manuscripts have continued to come to light throughout the past hundred years, particularly with the exploration of the two principal collections of his papers, one in Leningrad (see *39*) and the other the so-called Fonds Vandeul in the Bibliothèque Nationale in Paris (see *31*). As a result, earlier editions of Diderot's works are often inadequate and unreliable, as are the older critical studies. Further important modifications to critical judgements of Diderot have been made necessary by the major reassessment of the extent of his contribution to the *Encyclopédie*, by Professors Proust and Lough, and to the *Histoire des deux Indes*, by Michèle Duchet and others.

WORKS BY DIDEROT

By far the best collected edition, both for the text itself and for the critical apparatus, is the Hermann edition (*2*), though this is not yet complete. However, the four convenient 'Classiques Garnier' volumes (*3, 4, 5, 6*) contain most of Diderot's principal works, together with helpful critical apparatus.

1. *Œuvres complètes,* ed. J. Assézat and M. Tourneux, Paris, Garnier, 1875-77.
2. *Œuvres complètes,* ed. H. Dieckmann, J. Proust, J. Varloot, etc., Paris, Hermann, 1975- .
3. *Œuvres esthétiques,* ed. P. Vernière, Paris, 'Classiques Garnier', 1959.
4. *Œuvres philosophiques,* ed. P. Vernière, Paris, 'Classiques Garnier', 1961.
5. *Œuvres politiques,* ed. P. Vernière, Paris, 'Classiques Garnier', 1963.
6. *Œuvres romanesques,* ed. H. Bénac, Paris, 'Classiques Garnier', 1962.
7. *Supplément au voyage de Bougainville, Pensées philosophiques, Lettre sur les aveugles,* ed. A. Adam, Paris, Garnier Flammarion, 1972.
8. *Mémoires pour Catherine II,* ed. P. Vernière, Paris, Garnier, 1966.
9. *Correspondance,* ed. G. Roth and J. Varloot, Paris, Editions de Minuit, 1955-70.

The introduction and footnotes to the *Supplément* in *4* are extremely helpful, but the following separate editions of the work are most important:

10. Supplément au voyage de Bougainville, ed. G. Chinard, Paris, Droz, 1935.
11. Supplément au voyage de Bougainville, ed. H. Dieckmann, Geneva, Droz, and Lille, Giard, 1955.

The Chinard edition, based on the Leningrad manuscript, provides the definitive modern version of the text, and the introduction contains interesting background material, particularly concerning exploration in the Pacific and primitivism. The Dieckmann edition publishes an earlier manuscript, from the Fonds Vandeul, which contains important textual variants. It also has a most valuable critical introduction (to be supplemented, however, by *27*).

OTHER EIGHTEENTH-CENTURY WORKS

12. Bougainville, L.-A. de, *Voyage autour du monde,* ed. J. Proust, Paris, Gallimard ('Folio'), 1982.
13. Bricaire de La Dixmerie, N., *Le Sauvage de Taiti aux Français,* Paris, Lejay, 1770.
14. Raynal, G.Th., *Histoire philosophique et politique des deux Indes,* selections, ed. Y. Benot, Paris, Maspéro ('La Découverte'), 1981.
15. Rousseau, J.J., *Discours sur l'origine de l'inégalité,* in *Œuvres complètes,* Bibliothèque de la Pléiade, vol. III (1964).
16. Voltaire, *Candide,* in *Romans et contes,* ed. H. Bénac, Paris, 'Classiques Garnier', 1960.

BACKGROUND STUDIES

Among the great number of books and articles on the historical and anthropological background, the following, all of which contain material of direct relevance to the *Supplément,* are particularly useful:

17. Aldridge, A.O., 'The state of nature: an undiscovered country in the history of ideas', *Studies on Voltaire and the Eighteenth Century,* XCVIII (1972), pp.7-26.
18. Charlton, D.G., *New images of the natural in France – a study in European cultural history 1750-1800,* Cambridge, C.U.P., 1984.
19. Crocker, L.G., *Nature and culture: ethical thought in eighteenth-century France,* Baltimore, Johns Hopkins Press, 1963.
20. Duchet, M., *Anthropologie et histoire au siècle des lumières,* Paris, Maspéro, 1971.
21. Venturi, F., *Utopia and reform in the Enlightenment,* Cambridge, C.U.P., 1971.
22. White, Hayden, *Tropics of discourse: essays in cultural criticism,* Baltimore and London, Johns Hopkins Press, 1978. (Chapter 7: 'The forms of wildness' and Chapter 8: 'The noble savage as fetish'.)

GENERAL WORKS ON DIDEROT

There are many general works on Diderot, but the most useful for introductory reading are, in my opinion, the following:

23. Chouillet, J., *Diderot,* Paris, SEDES, 1977.
24. Crocker, L.G., *Diderot's chaotic order: approach to synthesis,*
    Princeton University Press, 1974.
25. France, P., *Diderot,* Oxford and New York, O.U.P. ('Past Masters'),
    1983.
26. Lefebvre, H., *Diderot,* Paris, Editeurs Réunis, 1949.

BOOKS AND ARTICLES DIRECTLY RELEVANT TO THE SUPPLEMENT

27. Belaval, Y., 'Nouvelles recherches sur Diderot', *Critique,* XIV, 107
    (April 1956), pp.291-318. (Review of *11,* pp.309-18.)
28. Benot, Y., *Diderot, de l'athéisme à l'anti-colonialisme,* Paris, Maspéro,
    1970.
29. Benrekassa, G.D., 'Dit et non-dit idéologique: à propos du *Supplément
    au voyage de Bougainville*', *Dix-huitième siècle,* V (1973), pp.29-40.
30. Booy, J. de, 'Inventaire provisoire des contributions de Diderot à la
    Correspondance littéraire', *Dix-huitième siècle,* I (1969), pp.353-97.
31. Dieckmann, H. *Inventaire du fonds Vandeul: inédits de Diderot,*
    Geneva, Droz, 1951.
32. Duchet, M., *Diderot et l'Histoire des deux-Indes ou l'Ecriture
    fragmentaire,* Paris, Nizet, 1978.
33. ——, 'Le primitivisme de Diderot', *Europe,* 405-06 (Jan-Feb. 1963),
    pp.126-37.
34. ——, 'Le *Supplément au voyage de Bougainville* et la collaboration de
    Diderot à l'*Histoire des Deux Indes*', CAIEF, XIII (1961), pp.173-87.
35. France, P. and Strugnell, A., ed., *Diderot: les dernières années, 1770-84,*
    Edinburgh University Press, 1985.
36. Giraud, Y., 'De l'exploration à l'utopie: notes sur la formation du
    mythe de Tahiti', *French Studies,* XXXI (Jan. 1977), pp.26-41.
37. Hall, M., *Benjamin Franklin and 'Polly Baker': the history of a literary
    deception,* Chapel Hill, University of North Carolina Press, 1960.
38. Hermand, P., *Les Idées morales de Diderot,* Paris, P.U.F., 1923.
39. Hoffmann, P., *La Femme dans la pensée des Lumières,* Paris, Ophrys,
    1977.
40. Johansson, J.V., *Etudes sur D. Diderot,* Göteborg and Paris,
    Champion, 1927.
40a. Leigh, R., 'Diderot's Tahiti', *Studies in the Eighteenth Century,* V
    (1983), pp.113-28.
41. Lough, J., 'The problem of the unsigned articles in the Encyclopédie',
    Studies on Voltaire and the Eighteenth Century, XXXII (1965),
    pp.327-90.

42. Loy, J.R., 'L'*Essai sur les règnes de Claude et de Néron*', *CAIEF*, XIII (1961), pp.239-54.

43. Perkins, M.L., 'Community planning in Diderot's *Supplément au voyage de Bougainville*', *Kentucky Romance Quarterly*, XXI (1974), pp.399-417.

44. Proust, J., *Diderot et l'Encyclopédie*, Paris, Armand Colin, 1967.

45. Sfragaro, A., 'La représentation de la femme chez Diderot', *Studies on Voltaire and the Eighteenth Century*, CXCIII (1980), pp.1893-99.

46. Sherman, C., *Diderot and the art of dialogue*, Geneva, Droz, 1976.

47. Spink, J.S., 'La vertu politique selon Diderot ou le paradoxe du bon citoyen', *Revue des sciences humaines*, CXII (Oct.-Dec. 1963), pp.471-83.

48. Strugnell, A., *Diderot's politics: a study of the evolution of Diderot's political thought after the Encyclopédie*, The Hague, Nijhoff, 1973.

49. Vianu, H., 'Nature et révolte dans la morale de Diderot', *Europe*, 405-06 (Jan.-Feb. 1963), pp.65-77.

50. Werner, S., 'Diderot's *Supplément* and the late Enlightenment thought', *Studies on Voltaire and the Eighteenth Century*, LXXXVI (1971), pp.229-92.

There are a number of other important articles, more or less relevant to the *Supplément*, in:

51. *Diderot Studies*, Syracuse University Press, then Geneva, Droz, 1949-

CRITICAL GUIDES TO FRENCH TEXTS

edited by

Roger Little, Wolfgang van Emden, David Williams